# Sustainable Sushi: 97 Delicious Plant-Based Recipes

De Urban Noodles

# Contents

# INTRODUCTION

Welcome to Sustainable Sushi: 97 Delicious Plant-Based Recipes, the ultimate guide for all things sushi! Whether you're a beginner in the art of sushi making or an experienced chef looking to explore different vegan sushi recipes, this cookbook will provide you with the perfect balance of creative recipes and simple instructions.

Sushi has been enjoyed as a delicacy around the world for centuries. Its recognisable flavour profile and presentation has made it a favourite amongst many. But sushi isn't just about fish; it can also be made from plant-based ingredients. This cookbook will provide you with an array of recipes to cater a variety of tastes, along with helpful suggestions that will easily guide you in creating your own masterpieces.

We'll explore vegan sushi recipes made with all kinds of vegetables, fruits, and other vegan ingredients. From classics like the Teriyaki Tempeh Roll, to full meals like the Dynamite Bowl, you'll find all types of delicious plant-based sushi.

Not only are these recipes tasty and imaginative, they're also sustainable. By focusing on plant-based ingredients, you'll be able to create sushi dishes that are kind to the environment and packed with essential nutrients. You'll also receive useful tips on how to source sustainable seafood ingredients and how to choose the best plant-based options.

From understanding the basics of sushi preparation to creating innovative vegan sushi dishes, Sustainable Sushi: 97 Delicious Plant-Based Recipes has everything you need to know. Get ready for an unforgettable journey into the world of sushi as you learn how to create culinary delights like no other!

# 1. Avocado Cucumber Roll

This is a tasty, light and refreshing recipe featuring avocado and cucumber. It makes for a perfect appetizer or side dish and is also a great vegan and gluten-free option.
Serving: 2 people
Preparation Time: 10 minutes
Ready Time: 10 minutes

**Ingredients:**
-1 large avocado, peeled and pitted
-1 large cucumber, cut into thin strips
-1 tablespoon of freshly squeezed lemon juice
-1 tablespoon of olive oil
-Salt and pepper, to taste

**Instructions:**
1. Place the avocado, cucumber strips, lemon juice, olive oil, salt and pepper in a bowl and gently mix them together until evenly combined.
2. Take one strip of the cucumber and use it to wrap a few pieces of the avocado in the center.
3. Continue to roll the cucumber and avocado until you have a cylindrical shape.
4. Serve immediately.

**Nutrition information:**
Calories Per Serving: 180; Fat: 14g; Carbohydrates: 11g; Protein: 3g

# 2. Vegan Spicy Tofu Roll

Craft a unique vegan dish to your table with this Vegan Spicy Tofu Roll. This yummy roll combines crispy tofu and a medley of vegetables with a delicious and spicy vegan sriracha mayonnaise.
Serving: Serves 4
Preparation Time: 15 minutes
Ready Time: 20 minutes

**Ingredients:**
-14 ounces of firm tofu sliced
-1 zucchini, thinly sliced lengthwise
-1 yellow squash, thinly sliced lengthwise
-1 tsp sesame oil
-2 tablespoons vegan sriracha mayonnaise
-3 tablespoons Tamari
-1 tablespoon olive oil

**Instructions:**
1. Preheat oven to 375 degrees F
2. Arrange the sliced tofu in a single layer on a greased baking sheet
3. Drizzle one tablespoon of olive oil over the tofu to lightly coat
4. Bake in preheated oven for 10 minutes, flipping once halfway through.
5. Remove tofu from oven and let cool
6. In a large bowl, combine the zucchini, yellow squash, sesame oil and Tamari. Mix until evenly coated
7. Heat a nonstick saute pan over medium-high heat
8. Place the zucchini and yellow squash mixture in pan and cook for 3-4 minutes. Stirring occasionally
9. Spread the vegan sriracha mayonnaise on the cooled tofu slices, and top with the cooked vegetables
10. Roll the tofu slices to form the Vegan Spicy Tofu Roll

**Nutrition information: Per serving -Calories 171kcal, Protein 8.9g, Carbohydrates 7.2g, Fat 11.5g, Saturated fat 1.7g, Sodium 454mg, Fiber 2.3g, Sugar 4.2g.**

## 3. Sweet Potato Tempura Roll

Sweet Potato Tempura Roll is a delicious and simple way to enjoy the flavor of sweet potatoes. It's a famous Japanese dish that is easy to make and perfect for a light evening meal.
Serving: 8-10
Preparation time: 10 minutes
Ready time: 45 minutes

**Ingredients:**

-2 cups of cooked sweet potato, sliced thin
-2 cups of white rice
-3 eggs
-3 tablespoons of sugar
-1/2 cup of panko bread crumbs
-1/2 teaspoon of salt
-1 cup of all-purpose flour
-3 cups of vegetable oil

**Instructions:**
1. Heat the vegetable oil in a large skillet over medium-high heat.
2. In a bowl, beat the eggs and sugar together until light and fluffy.
3. Place the all-purpose flour, panko bread crumbs, and salt into a separate shallow bowl and mix together.
4. Dip each sweet potato slice into the egg mixture and then into the flour mixture until fully coated.
5. Place each coated sweet potato slice into the hot oil and fry for 2-3 minutes per side, or until golden brown.
6. Drain the cooked sweet potato slices on a paper towel.
7. Place the cooked sweet potato slices onto the white rice and roll up.
8. Serve and enjoy!

**Nutrition information: Serving Size: 1 roll - Calories: 297, Fat: 10.3g, Saturated fat: 2.2g, Carbohydrates: 39.9g, Protein: 5.7g, Sodium: 276mg**

## 4. Mango and Avocado Roll

Try something new with this delicious combination of flavors: mango, avocado and lemony taste in this Mango and Avocado Roll.
Serving: 6
Preparation Time: 15 minutes
Ready Time: 25 minutes

**Ingredients:**
 4 large mangoes, peeled and cut into strips; 2 avocados, peeled and sliced; 2 tablespoons of freshly squeezed lemon juice; 6 sheets of nori

seaweed; 2 cups of cooked rice; 2 tablespoons of toasted sesame seeds; 1 tablespoon of finely chopped chives

**Instructions:**
1. To begin, place the cut mango and avocado strips on a sheet of nori seaweed.
2. Then sprinkle with lemon juice and set aside.
3. Heat a pan over medium heat and add the cooked rice. Stir frequently until it starts to become slightly toasted.
4. Add the toasted sesame seeds to the rice and stir until well combined.
5. Place a sheet of nori seaweed on a rolling mat, then spoon some of the rice mixture onto it.
6. Place the mango and avocado slices on top of the rice.
7. Gently roll the nori sheet up from one end to the other.
8. Secure the roll with a piece of kitchen twine and cut in half.
9. Repeat steps 5 through 8 with the remaining Ingredients.
10. Serve the rolls with some finely chopped chives for garnish.

**Nutrition information: (Serving Size: 1 roll) Calories: 145, Fat: 5.1 g, Carbohydrates: 23.1 g, Protein: 2.7 g, Sodium: 206 mg, Fiber: 3.9 g**


## 5. Vegan California Roll

This vegan version of the classic California Roll is perfect for all of your sushi cravings! It is filled with avocado, cucumber, and pickled radish for a delicious and nutritious plant-based meal.
Serving: 4 Rolls
Preparation Time: 15 minutes
Ready Time: 45 minutes

**Ingredients:**
- 2 sheets of nori
- 2 cups cooked sushi rice
- 1/2 teaspoon wasabi paste
- 2 tablespoons rice vinegar
- 2 tablespoons soy sauce
- 1 avocado, peeled and diced
- 1 cucumber, peeled and diced

- 1/4 cup pickled radish, diced

**Instructions:**
1. Cook the sushi rice according to the directions on the package and set aside.
2. In a small bowl, combine the wasabi paste, rice vinegar, and soy sauce and mix well.
3. Place the nori sheets on a flat surface.
4. Spread the sushi rice evenly onto each nori sheet.
5. Top each nori sheet with the diced avocado, cucumber, and pickled radish.
6. Drizzle each nori sheet with the wasabi sauce mixture.
7. Roll the nori sheets into tight cylinders.
8. Cut each roll into 4-6 slices.

**Nutrition information:**
Calories: 242 kcal
Carbohydrates: 38 g
Protein: 4 g
Fat: 8 g
Fiber: 4 g
Sodium: 435 mg

## 6. Vegan Teriyaki Mushroom Roll

Try this unique Vegan Teriyaki Mushroom Roll which is full of flavors. This roll has a mix of crunchiness and softness which makes it a delightful dish to have.
Serving: 4
Preparation Time : 10 minutes
Ready Time: 15 minutes

**Ingredients:**
• 8 sheets of dried nori
• 1/2 cup of teriyaki sauce
• 2 cups of cooked jasmine rice
• 2 tablespoons of sesame oil
• 2 cups of vegetable, such as carrots, peppers, mushrooms, diced

**Instructions:**
1. Preheat a large skillet over medium-high heat.
2. Add the vegetable mix and sesame oil and cook for 3 minutes or until the veggies start to soften.
3. Add teriyaki sauce and cook for a further 3 minutes, stirring to mix everything together.
4. Place a sheet of nori on a flat surface.
5. Spread 1/4 cup of cooked rice over the nori sheet.
6. Spoon 1/4 of the teriyaki vegetable mix over the rice.
7. Fold one side of the nori over the filling so the sides meet and roll lengthwise to make a roll.
8. Serve either warm or cold with extra teriyaki sauce on the side.

**Nutrition information: Total calories: 400 calories, Protein: 8g, Total fat: 7.5g, Saturated fat: 1.1g, Cholesterol: 0mg, Carbohydrate: 65g, Dietary fiber: 4g, Sodium: 1330mg**


## 7. Shiitake Mushroom and Asparagus Roll

Shiitake Mushroom and Asparagus Roll is a delicious Asian-style fusion dish that is flavorful and easy to make.
Serving: 4-6
Preparation time: 10 minutes
Ready time: 25 minutes

**Ingredients:**
· 12 Shiitake mushrooms, stemmed
· 12 asparagus spears
· 2 tablespoons olive oil
· 2 tablespoons tamari
· ½ teaspoon sesame oil
· 1 tablespoon grated ginger
· 1 teaspoon garlic, minced
· ½ teaspoon red pepper flakes
· Salt and pepper

**Instructions:**

1. Preheat the oven to 375°F.
2. Clean, dry, and stem the Shiitake mushrooms. Trim the asparagus to 2-3 inch long spears.
3. In a large bowl, combine the olive oil, tamari, sesame oil, ginger, garlic, and red pepper flakes.
4. Toss the mushrooms and asparagus in the marinade until well coated.
5. Arrange the mushrooms and asparagus on a baking sheet. Sprinkle with salt and pepper.
6. Bake in preheated oven for 20-25 minutes, until the mushrooms and asparagus are tender and browned.
7. Remove from oven, and let cool for a few minutes before serving.

**Nutrition information: Per Serving: Calories: 105, Protein: 3 g, Fat: 6 g, Carbohydrates: 10 g, Sodium: 294 mg, Fiber: 3 g.**


## 8. Vegan Spicy Mayo Roll

This vegan spicy mayo roll is a delicious combination of flavors featuring sushi-style seaweed rolls with a creamy vegan mayo and a spicy kick. A great way to please any crowd!
Serving: 4
Preparation time: 10 minutes
Ready time: 10 minutes

**Ingredients:**
- 4 sheets of sushi-ready seaweed
- 1/4 cup vegan mayonnaise
- 1 tablespoon sriracha chili sauce
- 2 cups cooked sushi rice

**Instructions:**
1. In a bowl, combine vegan mayo and sriracha chili sauce and mix until fully blended.
2. Lay a sheet of seaweed on a bamboo mat or counter.
3. Spread a thin layer of the mayo mixture over the seaweed sheet.
4. Spread 1/2 cup of the cooked sushi rice over the mayo layer.
5. Tightly roll the seaweed up, starting from the sides and rolling towards the middle.

6. Place the roll in a pan or bamboo mat and repeat steps 2-5 for remaining rolls.

7. Slice each roll into 4 equal pieces and serve.

**Nutrition information:**
- Calories: 196
- Fat: 7g
- Sodium: 381mg
- Carbohydrates: 28 g
- Protein: 4 g

## 9. Vegan Peanut Tofu Roll

This vegan peanut tofu roll is a delicious and healthy entrée. It's packed full of flavor, while being packed full of nutritional value thanks to crunchy veggies, rich peanut butter and protein-packed tofu.

Serving: 4-6

Preparation Time: 25 minutes

Ready Time: 55 minutes

**Ingredients:**
- 2 14oz packages extra-firm tofu
- 1/4 cup peanut butter
- 2 tablespoons sesame oil
- 2 tablespoons soy sauce
- 1 teaspoon garlic powder
- 1 teaspoon ground ginger
- 1 bell pepper, diced
- 1/2 cup shredded carrots
- 1/2 cup sliced mushrooms
- 1/4 cup chopped peanuts
- Salt and pepper to taste

**Instructions:**
1. Preheat oven to 400°F (200°C) and line a baking sheet with parchment paper.

2. Place blocks of tofu on cutting board. Wrap tofu in a few layers of paper towel to absorb excess liquid. Cut tofu lengthwise into four slices and then into cubes.

3. Combine peanut butter, sesame oil, soy sauce, garlic powder, and ginger in a large mixing bowl.

4. Add bell pepper, carrots, mushrooms, cubes of tofu, and peanuts to the bowl.

5. Add salt and pepper to taste and mix until Ingredients are evenly coated.

6. Spoon the mixture onto the parchment-lined baking sheet and spread out into an even layer.

7. Bake for 30 minutes, stirring occasionally to ensure even baking.

8. Serve tofu roll warm and top with additional chopped peanuts, if desired.

**Nutrition information:1 Serving= 232 calories; 13g fat; 16g carbohydrates; 10g protein**


# 10. Cucumber and Carrot Roll

Cucumber and Carrot Roll is a dish that is simple to prepare and delicious in taste. It is a combination of crunchy vegetables that can be served as an appetizer, a side dish or a snack.

Serving: 4

Preparation time: 15 minutes

Ready time: 35 minutes

**Ingredients:**
- 2 medium cucumbers
- 2 large carrots
- 4 teaspoons olive oil
- ½ teaspoon salt
- 2 tablespoons minced fresh parsley
- 2 tablespoons sesame seeds

**Instructions:**
1. Preheat the oven to 375°F.
2. Slice cucumbers and carrots into long, thin strips.

3. Place all vegetables in a medium bowl and toss with olive oil and salt.
4. Spread the vegetables on a foil-lined cookie sheet and bake in preheated oven for 20 minutes, stirring occasionally.
5. Remove the vegetables from the oven and sprinkle with parsley and sesame seeds.
6. Roll the vegetables into small rolls and serve.

**Nutrition information:**
Calories (per serving): 151 kcal, Carbohydrates: 17.6 g, Protein: 4.1 g, Fat: 8.3 g, Sodium: 368 mg, Dietary Fiber: 5.3 g

# 11. Vegan Dynamite Roll

Vegan Dynamite Roll is a delicious and vegan-friendly sushi roll that can be made at home with easily-accessible Ingredients.
Serving: 4
Preparation time: 15 minutes
Ready time: 30 minutes

**Ingredients:**
- 4 cups cooked white or brown sushi rice
- 1 avocado, sliced
- 1 red bell pepper, sliced into thin strips
- 4 sheets of Nori seaweed
- 1/4 cup vegan mayonnaise
- 1/4 cup sweet chili sauce

**Instructions:**
1. Cook sushi rice according to package directions. Let cool.
2. In a small bowl, combine vegan mayonnaise and sweet chili sauce and mix together.
3. Lay a sheet of Nori paper on a sushi mat.
4. Spread cooked sushi rice over the Nori paper, leaving a 1-inch border at the top.
5. Spread the mayonnaise-chili sauce mixture over the sushi rice.
6. Place slices of avocado and red bell pepper strips on top of the rice.
7. Roll the sushi up using the sushi mat. Make sure the top border of Nori paper is sealed.

8. Slice the sushi roll into 8 even pieces.

**Nutrition information: Per serving: 210 calories; 9 g fat; 28 g carbohydrates; 5 g protein.**

## 12. Vegan Tempura Vegetable Roll

Vegan Tempura Vegetable Roll is a delicious and healthy vegan dish which features lightly battered vegetables filled inside a savory roll. It's light, crunchy, and filled with comforting vegetables.
Serving: 6
Preparation time: 15 minutes
Ready time: 40 minutes

**Ingredients:**
- 2 carrots, julienne sliced
- 2 sweet potatoes, julienne sliced
- 1 red bell pepper, julienne sliced
- 1 cup vegan tempura mix
- ¾ cup vegan cold water
- 2 teaspoons avocado oil
- ½ teaspoon paprika
- 6 vegan sushi nori sheets

**Instructions:**
1. Preheat the oven to 350F/175C.
2. In a bowl, mix the tempura mix with cold water until combined.
3. Add the avocado oil and paprika. Mix until combined.
4. Dip the vegetables in the tempura batter one by one and place onto a baking sheet lined with parchment paper.
5. Bake the vegetables for 15 minutes until they are cooked through and golden.
6. To assemble the rolls, add the cooked vegetables onto the nori sheets.
7. Roll up the nori sheets leaving room for the vegetables inside.
8. Cut the rolls in half and serve.

**Nutrition information: per serving - Calories: 158, Fat: 4.9g, Carbohydrates: 23.6g, Protein: 5.4g**

# 13. Vegan Mango Tango Roll

Vegan mango tango roll is a delicious and delightful vegan sushi recipe. It is a wonderful combination of mango, avocado, and crunchy cucumber slices. It makes for a great lunch or light dinner.
Serving: 4 rolls
Preparation time: 30 minutes
Ready time: 30 minutes

**Ingredients:**
- 2 cups cooked sushi rice
- 4 sheets of nori (dry seaweed)
- 1 ripe mango, peeled and cut into thin slices
- 1 avocado, peeled and cut into thin slices
- 1/2 cucumber, peeled and cut into thin slices
- 2 tablespoons toasted sesame seeds
- Soy sauce, to serve

**Instructions:**
1. Place a sheet of nori seaweed, shiny side down, on a bamboo sushi mat.
2. Spread 1/2 cup cooked sushi rice on the nori.
3. Arrange the mango, avocado and cucumber slices in a line on the rice.
4. Sprinkle with sesame seeds and press lightly.
5. Roll the sushi firmly, using the mat for support.
6. Repeat with the remaining nori, rice, mango, avocado and cucumber.
7. Cut each roll into 8 pieces.
8. Serve with soy sauce.

**Nutrition information: per serving - 273 calories, 9.9g fat, 41.5g carbohydrates, 4.7g protein**

# 14. Vegan BBQ Tofu Roll

This vegan BBQ Tofu Roll is a delicious and easy dinner that you can make in no time!  With a tangy BBQ flavour, this vegan tofu roll is a dream for anyone looking for a tasty yet healthy meal.
Serving: 4
Preparation Time: 10 minutes
Ready Time: 20 minutes


**Ingredients:**
-1/2 block of extra-firm tofu
-1/2 cup BBQ sauce
-4 tortillas
-1/2 bell pepper, sliced
-1/4 cup minced onion
-4 tablespoons of olive oil
-2 tablespoons of parsley

**Instructions:**
1. Preheat oven to 350 degrees F.
2. Slice your block of tofu into 1/2 inch thick pieces.
3. In a bowl, combine the BBQ sauce with each of the tofu slices, making sure to coat each slice completely.
4. Add the bell peppers and onion to a skillet with the olive oil and cook for about 5 minutes.
5. Place the tofu slices onto the tortillas, top with bell peppers, onion and parsley.
6. Roll the tortillas up and place seam side down onto a baking dish.
7. Bake the tofu rolls in the oven for 12-15 minutes.

**Nutrition information:**
Serving Size: 2 roll ups
Calories: 260
Protein: 10 g
Carbohydrates: 28 g
Fat: 10 g


## 15. Sweet Potato and Avocado Roll

This Sweet Potato and Avocado Roll is packed with texture, flavor and nutrition. It is a great vegan snack that is low in carbs and rich in healthy fats and protein.

Serving: 8-10 rolls

Preparation time: 15 minutes

Ready Time: 30 minutes

**Ingredients:**

2 sweet potatoes

1 avocado

2 tablespoons olive oil

1 teaspoon cumin

1 teaspoon paprika

1/2 teaspoon garlic powder

sea salt and ground black pepper to taste

**Instructions:**

1. Begin by preheating oven to 400 degrees F. Slice each sweet potato lengthwise, into 16 even pieces. Arrange them on a lined baking sheet. Drizzle with olive oil, cumin, paprika, garlic powder, sea salt and black pepper.
2. Bake for about 20 minutes, until lightly browned and tender.
3. Once the sweet potatoes are finished baking, allow them to cool slightly.
4. Slice the avocado and spread a thin layer over each sweet potato slice.
5. Roll up the slices with the sliced avocado inside.
6. Serve and enjoy!

**Nutrition information**

Calories: 176

Fat: 12g

Carbohydrates: 15g

Protein: 4g

## 16. Vegan Crunchy Roll

This delicious vegan crunchy roll is a great savory snack with a crunchy texture. It's a great vegan option to enjoy and easy to prepare.

Serving: 4
Preparation Time: 15 mins
Ready Time: 40 mins

**Ingredients:**
- 2 tablespoons sesame oil
- 2 tablespoons light soy sauce
- 2 tablespoons rice vinegar
- Salt and black pepper, to taste
- 1 tablespoon cornstarch
- 1/2 teaspoon garlic powder
- 1/2 teaspoon ground ginger
- 1/4 teaspoon onion powder
- 2 cups cooked, cooled rice
- 4 sheets of nori (seaweed)
- 1/2 cup canned bamboo shoots, julienned
- 1/2 cup canned water chestnuts, julienned
- 1/4 cup carrots, julienned
- 1/4 cup bell peppers, julienned
- 1/4 cup green onions, chopped

**Instructions:**
1. Preheat oven to 375°F.
2. In a small bowl, whisk together sesame oil, soy sauce, rice vinegar, salt, black pepper, cornstarch, garlic powder, ground ginger and onion powder.
3. In a large bowl, mix together the cooked rice and the sesame oil mixture until evenly combined.
4. Place one sheet of nori on a baking sheet and spread the rice mixture onto the nori sheet.
5. Arrange the bamboo shoots, water chestnuts, carrots, bell peppers, and green onions on top of the rice.
6. Tightly roll the sheet up.
7. Repeat with the remaining sheets of nori.
8. Bake for 20 minutes and then turn over and bake for an additional 10 minutes.
9. Slice into 1-inch pieces and serve.

**Nutrition information:**

Calories: 156, Fat: 5.8g, Carbohydrates: 24.3g, Protein: 2.6g, Sodium: 843.2mg, Fiber: 1.2g.

## 17. Vegan Teriyaki Eggplant Roll

This delicious vegan teriyaki eggplant roll is the perfect addition to any meal! This vegan dish uses eggplant, sesame oil, garlic, and teriyaki sauce to create an Asian-inspired vegan delight that is sure to please everyone.
Serving: Serves 6-8
Preparation time: 15 minutes
Ready Time: 45 minutes

**Ingredients:**
- 1 large eggplant, cut lengthwise into 8 thick slices
- 2 tablespoons sesame oil
- 2 cloves of garlic, minced
- 2/3 cup teriyaki sauce
- 2 tablespoons toasted sesame seeds

**Instructions:**
1. Preheat oven to 400°F.
2. Place the eggplant slices on a lightly greased baking sheet. Drizzle sesame oil over the eggplant and spread evenly. Top with garlic and bake for 25 minutes.
3. Once eggplant is cooked, brush each slice with teriyaki sauce and sprinkle with toasted sesame seeds. Bake for an additional 15 minutes.
4. Serve the eggplant rolls warm.

**Nutrition information**
Calories: 90, Total Fat: 4.5g, Saturated Fat: 0.5g, Cholesterol: 0mg, Sodium: 300mg, Carbohydrates: 11g, Fiber: 3.5g, Sugars: 6g, Protein: 2.5g

## 18. Shiitake Mushroom and Cucumber Roll

This dish combines two fresh Ingredients – Shiitake mushrooms and cucumber – to create a delicious roll that can be enjoyed as a snack, side dish or appetizer. It is a bright and flavorful recipe that is easy to make and takes little time to prepare.

Serving: 6
Preparation Time: 10 minutes
Ready Time: 20 minutes

**Ingredients:**
- 10 medium-sized shiitake mushrooms
- 2 cucumbers
- 1 teaspoon minced garlic
- 2 tablespoons olive oil
- 1 teaspoon sesame oil
- 1 teaspoon sesame seeds
- 2 teaspoons soy sauce
- Salt and pepper, to taste

**Instructions:**
1. Slice the shiitake mushrooms and cucumbers into thin strips.
2. Heat the olive oil in a large skillet over medium-high heat.
3. Add garlic and stir for 1 minute.
4. Add mushrooms and cucumber strips and season with salt and pepper to taste.
5. Cook until mushrooms and cucumber are lightly browned, about 5 minutes.
6. In a small bowl, mix together sesame oil, sesame seeds, and soy sauce.
7. Add the sesame mixture to the skillet and stir to combine.
8. Remove from heat and let cool.
9. To assemble the rolls, lay out several strips of mushrooms and cucumber, overlapping slightly.
10. Roll up the strips and place on a plate.
11. Serve.

**Nutrition information:**
Serving size: 1 roll
Calories: 71
Fat: 4g
Carbohydrates: 4g
Protein: 2g
Fiber: 1g

# 19. Vegan Green Dragon Roll

This Vegan Green Dragon Roll is a healthy and tasty vegan sushi roll with cucumber, avocado, and spicy sprouts. It's a great meal to serve as an appetizer or as a light meal.
Serving: 4 rolls
Preparation time: 10 minutes
Ready time: 10 minutes

**Ingredients:**
- 4 nori seaweed sheets
- 2 cups cooked sushi rice
- 1 avocado, peeled and sliced
- 1 cucumber, seeded and sliced
- 1 cup spicy sprouts
- 2 tablespoons toasted sesame seeds
- vegan soy sauce, for Serving:

**Instructions:**
1. Lay a seaweed sheet on a wooden sushi mat and spread a thin layer of cooked sushi rice on the left two-thirds of the sheet.
2. Arrange the sliced avocado, cucumber, and spicy sprouts along the middle of the sushi rice, leaving half an inch of seaweed exposed at the ends.
3. Sprinkle the toasted sesame seeds over the vegetables.
4. Starting from the top of the seaweed sheet, use the sushi mat to tightly roll the sushi into a cylindrical shape.
5. Slice the roll into 1-inch pieces.
6. Serve with vegan soy sauce.

**Nutrition information:**
- Calories per roll: 130
- Fat per roll: 5 g
- Protein per roll: 2 g
- Carbohydrates per roll: 18 g

# 20. Vegan Spicy Vegetable Roll

Vegan Spicy Vegetable Roll is a delicious and healthy vegan dish with an aromatic and unique flavor. It is a combination of cooked veggies mixed with fragrant spices wrapped in rice paper for a great crunchy bite.
Serving: 4 pieces
Preparation Time: 15 minutes
Ready Time: 20 minutes

**Ingredients:**
- ½ cup cabbage, finely shredded
- ½ cup carrots, grated
- ½ cup cucumber, finely chopped
- 1 green onion, finely chopped
- ½ red pepper, diced
- ¼ cup fresh cilantro, finely chopped
- 1 teaspoon of olive oil
- ½ teaspoon chili powder
- Salt and ground pepper to taste
- 4 rice papers
- ¼ cup vegan mayonnaise

**Instructions:**
1. In a large bowl, combine cabbage, carrots, cucumber, green onion, red pepper, cilantro, olive oil, chili powder, salt and pepper to taste. Mix all Ingredients until well combined.
2. Dip each rice paper in warm water for about 10 seconds until soft and pliable.
3. Place the rice paper on a flat surface and spread the prepared vegetables evenly across the center.
4. Roll up the rice paper, tucking both ends in.
5. Serve the rolls with a side of vegan mayonnaise.

**Nutrition information:**
Calories: 199, Fat: 9g, Carbs: 24g, Protein: 4g, Fiber: 4g, Sodium: 231mg

# 21. Avocado and Asparagus Roll

Avocado and Asparagus Roll is a delectable vegan appetizer that is simple to make and full of flavor.

Serving: 10 sushi rolls

Preparation time: 15 minutes

Ready time: 20 minutes

**Ingredients:**
- 10 sheets of sushi nori
- 2 ripe avocados, cut into thin strips
- 10 asparagus spears, cut into thin strips
- 2 tablespoons mashed avocado
- 2 tablespoons cooked brown rice
- Soy sauce, to taste

**Instructions:**
1. Place a sheet of sushi nori on your work surface. Using wet, clean hands, spread one tablespoon of mashed avocado evenly over the nori.
2. Place one asparagus spear in the center of the nori sheet and top with two thin strips of avocado.
3. Roll into a tight log and cut into 5 equal sushi rolls.
4. Place the sushi rolls onto a serving platter and serve with soy sauce.

**Nutrition information:**
Calories: 120 kcal, Protein: 3g, Total Fat: 7g, Total Carbohydrate: 12g, Dietary Fiber: 4g, Sugars: 1g, Sodium: 160mg

## 22. Vegan Rainbow Roll

Get your vitamin boost with this delicious vegan rainbow roll! Filled with a rainbow of colorful vegetables and wrapped in sushi rice and seaweed, it's sure to be a hit with vegan and non-vegans alike.

Serving: 4

Preparation time: 15 minutes

Ready time: 25 minutes

**Ingredients:**
- 1 sheet of nori seaweed
- 2 cups cooked sushi rice

- 2 carrots, grated or cut into thin strips
- 2 bell peppers, sliced or cut into thin strips
- 1 cucumber, sliced or cut into thin strips
- 1 avocado, cut into thin strips
- 1/4 cup sesame seeds
- Soy sauce or tamari for dipping

**Instructions:**
1. Place the nori sheet on a sushi mat and spread the cooked sushi rice over the top.
2. Arrange the carrots, bell peppers, cucumber and avocado in a line down the center of the sushi sheet.
3. Sprinkle the sesame seeds over the vegetables.
4. Carefully roll up the sushi roll using the sushi mat.
5. Cut the rolled sushi into 8 equal pieces and serve with soy sauce or tamari for dipping. Enjoy!

**Nutrition information:**
Calories: 211; Total Fat: 8g; Saturated Fat: 1g; Sodium: 275mg; Total Carbohydrate: 27g; Dietary Fiber: 5g; Protein: 7g.

## 23. Vegan Teriyaki Seitan Roll

Vegan Teriyaki Seitan Roll is a tasty and healthy vegan meal. It is made using seitan, a protein-rich ingredient made from wheat gluten, along with delicious teriyaki sauce and vegetables.
Serving: 2
Preparation time: 25 minutes
Ready time: 45 minutes

**Ingredients:**
- 1 cup seitan, cubed
- 1 cup carrots, shredded
- 1/2 cup green onions, diced
- 1/4 cup teriyaki sauce
- 2 sheets of vegan-friendly seaweed

**Instructions:**

1. Preheat the oven to 375°F.
2. In a large bowl, mix together the seitan, carrots, and green onions.
3. In a separate bowl, mix together the teriyaki sauce and 2 tablespoons of water.
4. Grease a baking sheet.
5. Place a sheet of seaweed on the baking sheet.
6. Spread the seitan mixture onto the sheet of seaweed.
7. Drizzle the teriyaki sauce mixture over the seitan.
8. Top with the second seaweed sheet.
9. Roll the seaweed up, starting at one end.
10. Place the roll on the baking sheet and bake for 15 minutes.
11. Cut into slices and serve.

**Nutrition information:**
Calories: 205, Total Fat: 4g, Saturated Fat: 0.6g, Cholesterol: 0mg, Sodium: 716mg, Carbohydrates: 16g, Fiber: 5.7g, Protein: 25.1g

## 24. Vegan Tempura Sweet Potato Roll

This vegan tempura sweet potato roll has a deliciously crisp texture on the outside with a creamy, comforting filling on the inside. It's a great dish to serve as an appetizer, party treat, or side dish.
Serving: This recipe serves 4 people.
Preparation time: 45 minutes
Ready time: 1 hour

**Ingredients:**
• 3 sweet potatoes (350g)
• 200g all-purpose flour
• 1 teaspoon baking powder
• 200ml non-dairy milk, cold
• Vegetable oil, for deep-frying
• Salt, to taste

**Instructions:**
1. Peel the sweet potatoes and cut into slices.
2. In a bowl, combine the flour, baking powder, and non-dairy milk and whisk to make a batter.

3. Heat vegetable oil in a deep fryer or heavy-bottomed pan.
4. Dip each sweet potato slice into the batter and deep-fry until golden-brown.
5. Drain on paper towels before serving.
6. Sprinkle with salt to taste.

**Nutrition information:**
Calories 69, Protein 2g, Total Fat 2g, Cholesterol 0mg, Sodium 2mg, Total Carbohydrate 11g, Fiber 2g, Sugar 4g

## 25. Mango and Cucumber Roll

Mango and Cucumber Roll – a delicious spring and summer appetizer or snack combination that is light and quick to make.
Serving: 2
Preparation Time: 15 minutes
Ready Time: 15 minutes

**Ingredients:**
- 2 Cucumbers
- 2 Mango, peeled and cut into strips
- 1/4 cup Mayo
- 2 teaspoons Lime Juice
- Salt and Pepper to taste
- Handful of Cilantro Leaves (optional)

**Instructions:**
1. Peel and slice the cucumbers into thin slices.
2. Meanwhile, peel and cut the mango into thin strips.
3. In a bowl, mix together the mayo, lime juice, salt, and pepper.
4. Place a strip of the mango onto a cucumber slice, and attach it with a tiny bit of the mayo mixture.
5. Continue with this process until all the cucumber slices are covered with mango.
6. Top with some cilantro leaves (optional).

**Nutrition information: Per Serving (serving size of 2): Calories: 210, Total Fat: 12g, Saturated Fat: 2g, Cholesterol: 6mg, Sodium: 410mg, Total Carbohydrate: 21g, Dietary Fiber: 2g, Protein: 2g.**

## 26. Vegan Philadelphia Roll

This vegan Philadelphia Roll is a flavorful sushi roll that is protein-packed and a great dinner option. It uses vegan cream cheese in place of the traditional Philadelphia Roll's raw fish.
Serving: Makes 2 rolls (8 pieces).
Preparation Time: 10 minutes
Ready Time: 20 minutes

**Ingredients:**
- 2 sheets nori
- 2/3 cup cooked, sushi rice (white or brown)
- ½ avocado
- 2 tablespoons vegan cream cheese
- 2 tablespoons capers
- 2 teaspoons chopped chives
- 2 teaspoons toasted sesame seeds

**Instructions:**
1. Place the nori onto a sushi mat or flat surface.
2. Spread the sushi rice over the nori.
3. Slice the avocado into thin slices.
4. Spread the cream cheese, capers, and chives over the top of the sushi rice.
5. Sprinkle with sesame seeds and place the avocado slices on top.
6. Roll the sushi up and use the sushi mat to form it into a tight roll.
7. Slice the roll into 8 pieces.

**Nutrition information:**
Calories: 279; Protein: 4 grams; Carbs: 35 grams; Fat: 13 grams.

## 27. Vegan Peanut Avocado Roll

Vegan Peanut Avocado Rolls are delicious and healthy vegan rolls packed with crunchy peanut and creamy avocado.
Serving: 4-6
Preparation Time: 20 minutes
Ready Time: 40 minutes

**Ingredients:**
- 1/2 cup of peanuts
- 2 ripe avocados
- 2 tablespoons of coconut cream
- 2 tablespoons of vegan mayonnaise
- 1 teaspoon of sesame oil
- 4 wraps

**Instructions:**
1. Preheat the oven to 350F.
2. Spread the peanuts onto a baking sheet and bake for about 10 minutes.
3. Peel and pit the avocados and place them in a bowl. Mash the avocados with a fork until they reach a smoother consistency.
4. Add the coconut cream, vegan mayonnaise, and sesame oil to the mashed avocados and stir until combined.
5. Once the peanuts are finished baking, add them to the avocado mixture stirring to combine.
6. Lay out the wraps and spread the peanut avocado mixture evenly on each one.
7. Roll the wrap up tightly.
8. Cut each wrap into 1 inch pieces and serve.

**Nutrition information: (Per Serving)**
Calories: 246 kcal
Carbohydrates: 19 g
Protein: 6 g
Fat: 16 g
Fiber: 5 g
Sugar: 2 g

# 28. Vegan Spicy Tofu Tempura Roll

This vegan-friendly spicy tofu tempura roll is an easy-to-make sushi that packs a delicious punch of savory and spicy flavors. It is sure to be a hit with your vegan and non-vegan friends alike!

Serving: 1
Preparation Time: 20 minutes
Ready Time: 20 minutes

**Ingredients:**
-1/2 block extra-firm tofu, cut into thin strips
-1/4 cup all-purpose flour
-1/4 cup water
-1 cup panko breadcrumbs
-1 teaspoon of chili powder
-1 teaspoon of garlic powder
-1 teaspoon of onion powder
-1 teaspoon of cumin
-1 teaspoon of pepper
-Oil, for frying

**Instructions:**
1. Start by heating the oil in a deep pan for about 5 minutes.
2. Meanwhile, make the tempura batter by mixing the flour and the water until it is lump-free.
3. Place the panko breadcrumbs in a shallow dish and add the chili powder, garlic powder, onion powder, cumin, and pepper to it.
4. Dip each piece of tofu in the tempura batter, and then the seasoned panko breadcrumbs.
5. Carefully place each piece of tofu in the hot oil and fry for about 1 minute, or until golden brown.
6. Remove from the oil and place on a paper towel-lined plate to catch excess oil.
7. Once all the tofu is fried, assemble the sushi roll!

**Nutrition information: Per Serving: Calories: 380, Total Fat: 15g, Saturated Fat: 3g, Cholesterol: 0mg, Sodium: 660mg, Total Carbohydrates: 42g, Dietary Fiber: 6.7g, Sugar: 3.2g, Protein: 20.3g**

# 29. Vegan Crunchy Spicy Mayo Roll

Vegan Crunchy Spicy Mayo Roll is a delicious vegan-friendly snack made from crunchy mayonnaise with a hint of spice. This tasty snack will be sure to please the entire family.

Serving: 4

Preparation time: 10 minutes

Ready time: 25 minutes

**Ingredients:**

2 tablespoons vegan mayonnaise

2 tablespoons vegan chili sauce

1 teaspoon garlic powder

1 teaspoon onion powder

1 teaspoon paprika

2 cups vegan, gluten-free bread crumbs

1 tablespoon olive oil

**Instructions:**

1. Preheat oven to 350 degrees F.

2. In a medium bowl, mix together mayonnaise, chili sauce, garlic powder, onion powder, and paprika.

3. Place bread crumbs in a separate bowl.

4. Dip the vegan roll in the mayonnaise mixture, then roll in the bread crumbs to coat.

5. Place on a greased baking sheet and bake for 12 minutes, or until golden brown.

6. Drizzle with olive oil and serve.

**Nutrition information: Per serving (4 servings): Calories: 270; Total Fat: 9g; Sodium: 450mg; Carbohydrates: 34g; Protein: 5g.**

# 30. Vegan Teriyaki Portobello Roll

Vegan Teriyaki Portobello Roll is a delicious and flavorful dish! This recipe is the perfect vegan dinner or lunch with an Asian twist. It is full of flavor, texture, and fresh Ingredients.

Serving - Serves 2

Preparation Time - 10 minutes
Ready Time - 30 minutes

**Ingredients:**
- 4 portobello mushrooms
- 3 tablespoons vegan teriyaki sauce
- 1/4 cup teriyaki glaze
- 1 teaspoon garlic powder
- 1 teaspoon ginger powder
- 2 tablespoons olive oil
- 4 nori sheets
- 1 teaspoon black sesame
- 1 tablespoon soy sauce
- 1 tablespoon honey
- 2 cups cooked jasmine rice

**Instructions:**
1. Preheat oven to 350°F/180°C.
2. Clean the portobello mushrooms with a damp cloth, and brush with some olive oil.
3. Place the mushrooms on a baking tray, and bake in the oven for 10-15 minutes until they are cooked and tender.
4. In a bowl, mix together the teriyaki sauce, teriyaki glaze, garlic powder, ginger powder, and a drizzle of olive oil.
5. Once the mushrooms are done baking, brush them with the teriyaki sauce and glaze mixture.
6. Place a nori sheet on a flat surface. Spread 1/2 cup of cooked jasmine rice on the nori sheet.
7. Place one mushroom on top of the rice and top with some black sesame, soy sauce, and honey.
8. Roll the nori sheet and rice around the mushroom.
9. Place the rolls on a baking tray and repeat with the remaining mushrooms.
10. Bake for 10-15 minutes until the rolls are golden and crispy.
11. Serve with extra teriyaki sauce and enjoy!

**Nutrition information**
Per serving - 656 calories, 11 g fat, 131 g carbohydrates, 32 g protein

# 31. Vegan Tempura Asparagus Roll

This Vegan Tempura Asparagus Roll is a delicious twist on a classic sushi roll. It is sure to satisfy your vegan and non-vegan friends alike with its wonderful combination of crisp tempura-fried asparagus and sticky sushi rice.

Serving: This recipe makes 2 tempura asparagus rolls, which serves 2 people.

Preparation time: 20 minutes

Ready Time: 1 hour

**Ingredients:**
- 1 tsp sesame oil
- 8 fresh asparagus spears
- 2-3 cups vegetable oil (for frying)
- 1 cup all-purpose flour
- 2 cups panko breadcrumbs
- 1 cup sushi rice
- 2 sheets of nori seaweed
- 2 tbsp vegan mayonnaise

**Instructions:**
1. In a medium pan, heat the sesame oil over medium heat. Add the asparagus and sauté for 2-3 minutes, then remove from heat.
2. Heat the vegetable oil in a large pot over medium high heat.
3. In a shallow bowl, combine the flour and panko together.
4. Dip the asparagus in the flour/panko mixture to coat.
5. Fry the asparagus in the hot oil until golden brown, about 2-3 minutes. Remove from the oil and drain on paper towels.
6. In a medium pan, cook the sushi rice according to package instructions.
7. Place a sheet of nori on a sushi mat. Top with the sushi rice and spread evenly, leaving a 2-inch border at the top and bottom.
8. Place the tempura asparagus in the middle of the sushi rice, and spread a thin layer of vegan mayonnaise over the asparagus.
9. Starting from the bottom of the sheet, roll the sushi tightly.
10. Slice into 8 pieces with a sharp knife and serve.

**Nutrition information**
Per serving:

Calories: 554
Fat: 39.2 g
Carbs: 37.7 g
Protein: 14.5 g

## 32. Vegan Mango and Jalapeno Roll

This vegan mango and jalapeno roll is made with fresh mangos, vegan
cream cheese and spicy jalapenos for a perfect summer wrap.
Serving: 8 wraps
Preparation Time: 15 minutes
Ready Time: 30 minutes

**Ingredients:**
• 8 Wonton wrappers
• 2 ripe mangos (diced)
• 4 oz vegan cream cheese
• 2 jalapenos (diced)
• 2 tablespoons vegan mayonnaise
• Sea salt to taste

**Instructions:**
1. In a small bowl, mix together the mango, vegan cream cheese,
jalapenos, vegan mayonnaise and salt until well combined.
2. Place a wonton wrapper on a flat surface and spread 1 tablespoon of
the vegan cream cheese mixture on the upper center of the wrapper.
3. Fold the bottom corner of the wrapper up to meet the top corner.
Then fold each side corner in and press gently to seal the edges together.
4. Repeat these steps with the remaining wrappers and filling.
5. Heat a large skillet over low heat and add the rolls. cook for 2-3
minutes per side, or until the wonton wrapper is golden brown and
crispy.
6. Serve hot or cold, accompanied with your favorite dipping sauce.

**Nutrition information:**
Serving size: 1 wrap
Calories: 71
Fat:1.5 g

Carbohydrates: 11.3 g
Protein: 1.8 g

## 33. Vegan BBQ Mushroom Roll

Vegan BBQ Mushroom Roll is an easy to make and delicious appetizer that only requires a few Ingredients. It is warm and cheesy, and perfect for your next party or gathering!
Serving: 8-10 rolls
Preparation time: 20 minutes
Ready time: 20 minutes

**Ingredients:**
- 8-10 whole wheat tortillas
- 2 tablespoons olive oil
- 1 cup BBQ sauce
- 1/2 onion, diced
- 1 cup mushrooms, diced
- 1/4 cup nutritional yeast
- 2 cups cooked kidney beans, mashed
- Salt and pepper, to taste

**Instructions:**
1. Preheat oven to 375 degrees F.
2. Heat oil in a skillet over medium-high heat and add onions. Cook, stirring occasionally, until softened, about 5 minutes.
3. Add mushrooms and cook for an additional 2-3 minutes, until mushrooms are cooked through.
4. Add BBQ sauce and cook for another 2 minutes, stirring occasionally.
5. Remove from heat and stir in kidney beans and nutritional yeast. Mix until combined.
6. Place a spoonful of the mixture onto each tortilla and carefully roll up each one. Secure with toothpicks if needed.
7. Place the rolls on a baking sheet and bake for 10 minutes.

**Nutrition information:**
Serving size - 1 roll
Calories - 137

Total Fat - 3.6g
Saturated Fat - 0.8g
Carbohydrates - 19.4g
Fiber - 3.9g
Sugar - 5.9g
Protein - 6.5g

# 34. Avocado and Radish Roll

Avocado and Radish Rolls are a delicious and light Vietnamese-style appetizer featuring crunchy radishes and creamy avocado encased in a delicate rice paper wrap and served with a dipping sauce.
Serving: 4
Preparation Time: 10 minutes
Ready Time: 10 minutes

**Ingredients:**
- 10-12 round rice paper wrappers
- 2 large ripe avocados
- 8-10 radishes
- 2 tablespoons lime juice
- 1 teaspoon sea salt
- A small bowl of warm water

**Instructions:**
1. Slice the radishes into thin matchsticks and place in a medium bowl with the lime juice and salt. Stir to combine.
2. Pit the avocados and cut into thin slices.
3. Dip a rice paper wrapper in the warm water for a few seconds until soft and pliable, then lay on a clean surface.
4. Place a few pieces of radish and avocado in the middle of the wrapper and roll up from the bottom, tucking in the sides as you go.
5. Repeat with the remaining wrappers.
6. Serve with a dipping sauce of choice.

**Nutrition information: (Per Serving)**
- Calories: 181
- Fat: 11g

- Carbohydrates: 24g
- Protein: 3g
- Sodium: 455 mg
- Cholesterol: 0mg
- Fiber: 5g

## 35. Vegan Dynamite Spicy Mayo Roll

Vegan Dynamite Spicy Mayo Roll is a delicious and creative vegan roll with a Japanese-style spicy mayonnaise. It's light, flavorful, and perfect for summer.
Serving: 4
Preparation time: 10 minutes
Ready time: 10 minutes

**Ingredients:**
- Nori sheets
- Sushi rice
- Shiitake mushrooms
- Avocado
- Green onion
- Sriracha
- Japanese mayonnaise

**Instructions:**
1. Place nori sheet flat on a surface.
2. Spread a ½ cup of cooked sushi rice evenly in the middle of the nori sheet.
3. Top the rice with 2 thinly sliced, cooked shiitake mushrooms.
4. Slice one avocado in half and slice each half into ¼ in. strips, then layer the avocado over the mushrooms.
5. Finely chop one green onion and sprinkle it over the avocado.
6. Drizzle a generous amount of Sriracha over top of the avocado and green onion.
7. Place one tablespoon of Japanese mayonnaise in the center of the nori sheet.

8. Begin rolling up the nori sheet starting at the end closest to you towards the top. As you roll, use your fingers to press any loose Ingredients back into the roll. Make sure to roll it tightly for best results.
9. Once the roll is complete, use a sharp knife to cut into four pieces.

**Nutrition information:**
Calories: 204, Total Fat: 11g, Saturated Fat: 1g, Cholesterol: 0mg, Sodium: 350mg, Total Carbohydrates: 21g, Dietary Fiber: 3g, Sugars: 1g, Protein: 4g.

## 36. Vegan Sweet Potato Tempura Roll

Enjoy this vegan sweet potato tempura roll that's full of flavor and crunch. It's a delicious gluten-free main dish or appetizer that is sure to be a hit!
Scrving: 4
Preparation time: 10 minutes
Ready time: 25 minutes

**Ingredients:**
- 1 large sweet potato, peeled and sliced into thin strips
- 1/2 cup white rice flour
- 1/2 cup cornstarch
- 1 teaspoon garlic powder
- 1 teaspoon baking powder
- 1 teaspoon chili powder
- 1/2 teaspoon salt
- 2 cups vegetable oil, for frying

**Instructions:**
1. Heat the vegetable oil in a large skillet over medium-high heat.
2. In a medium bowl, mix together the white rice flour, cornstarch, garlic powder, baking powder, chili powder, and salt.
3. Dip the sliced sweet potato strips in the flour mixture and then carefully place in the hot oil.
4. Fry the sweet potato strips until they are golden brown, about 3 minutes per side.

5. Remove the sweet potato tempura strips from the oil and place on a paper towel-lined plate to drain.
6. Serve with your favorite dipping sauce and enjoy!

**Nutrition information:**
Serving size: 1/4 of recipe
Calories: 132
Fat: 8 g
Saturated fat: 1 g
Carbohydrates: 14 g
Protein: 1 g
Sodium: 154 mg
Fiber: 1 g

# 37. Vegan Teriyaki Tofu and Cucumber Roll

Enjoy the delicious taste of a Vegan Teriyaki Tofu and Cucumber Roll in just a few short steps. This roll is a great healthy option that can be enjoyed as either an appetizer or light meal.
Serving: 6
Preparation Time: 10 minutes
Ready Time: 30 minutes

**Ingredients:**
- 12 ounces extra-firm tofu
- ¼ cup teriyaki sauce
- 2 tablespoons vegetable oil
- ½ teaspoon salt
- 1 cup sliced cucumber
- ½ cup prepared sushi rice
- 3 tablespoons toasted sesame seeds
- 2 teaspoons brown sugar
- 6 sheets nori seaweed

**Instructions:**
1. Drain the tofu and pat it dry with paper towels. Cut the block into 6 pieces.

2. In a small bowl, combine the teriyaki sauce, vegetable oil, salt, and brown sugar. Add the tofu to the bowl and toss until it's coated. Let it marinate for 15 minutes.
3. Preheat the oven to 400°F. Line a baking sheet with parchment paper. Arrange the tofu on the baking sheet and brush with the remaining marinade.
4. Bake the tofu for 20 minutes, flipping the pieces halfway through.
5. To assemble the roll: Spread the sushi rice onto each sheet of seaweed. Place a piece of tofu and cucumber slices in the middle and sprinkle with sesame seeds. Roll up the seaweed and secure the ends with a toothpick.
6. Cut each roll into 8 pieces and serve.

**Nutrition information: Servings: 6 | Calories: 207 kcal | Carbohydrates: 13.9 g | Protein: 7.2 g | Fat: 14.2 g | Saturated Fat: 8.9 g | Sodium: 620 mg | Potassium: 121 mg | Fiber: 0.3 g | Sugar: 5.5 g | Vitamin C: 0.2 mg | Calcium: 44 mg | Iron: 0.9 mg**

## 38. Vegan Shiitake Mushroom and Avocado Roll

This vegan shiitake mushroom and avocado roll is an easy and healthy appetizer to whip up for any occasion. It's full of flavor and crunch and is sure to be a hit at your dinner table!
Serving: 6
Preparation time: 15 mins
Ready time: 15 mins

**Ingredients:**
- 6 nori sheets
- 6 tablespoons cooked sushi rice
- 1 ripe avocado, peeled and sliced
- 12-15 shiitake mushrooms, sliced
- 2 tablespoons white sesame seeds
- 2 tablespoons black sesame seeds

**Instructions:**
1. Start by prepping your Ingredients. Peel and slice the avocado and the shiitake mushrooms.
2. Place a nori sheet on a cutting board or on a sushi mat.

3. Spread about 1 tablespoon of cooked sushi rice onto the nori sheet.
4. Layer the avocado and shiitake mushrooms on top.
5. Sprinkle with white and black sesame seeds.
6. Roll up the sushi tightly and cut it into 6 pieces.
7. Repeat steps 2 through 6 with the other nori sheets.

**Nutrition information: A serving of vegan Shiitake Mushroom and Avocado Roll contains approximately 190 calories. It is a good source of Vitamin E, vitamin C, vitamin K, calcium and dietary fiber. It is also a good source of healthy fats and proteins.**

## 39. Vegan Spicy Peanut Roll

This Vegan Spicy Peanut Roll is the perfect combination of sweet, savory, and spicy all in one delicious bite! Enjoy the fabulous blend of flavors with the convenience of a flavorful and healthy vegan roll.
Serving: Makes 8 rolls
Preparation Time: 10 minutes
Ready Time: 40 minutes

**Ingredients:**
- 1 sheet of thawed vegan puff pastry
- 2 tablespoons olive oil
- 2 tablespoons sesame seeds
- 2 tablespoons maple syrup
- 2 tablespoons sriracha
- 2 tablespoons peanut butter

**Instructions:**
1. Preheat oven 425°F. Line a baking sheet with parchment paper.
2. Unfold the thawed vegan puff pastry onto the prepared baking sheet. Brush the pastry evenly with olive oil.
3. Sprinkle sesame seeds over the pastry, followed by maple syrup, sriracha, and peanut butter.
4. Roll pastry up from the longest end and using a sharp knife, cut pastry into 1-inch pieces.
5. Bake for 20 minutes, flip the rolls and bake for an additional 20 minutes.

6. Enjoy the spicy peanut rolls warm or cooled.

**Nutrition information (per serving):**
Calories: 297 kcal, Carbohydrates: 30 g, Protein: 5 g, Fat: 17 g, Saturated
Fat: 3 g, Sodium: 133 mg, Potassium: 68 mg, Fiber: 1 g, Sugar: 12 g,
Vitamin A: 1 IU, Calcium: 11 mg, Iron: 1 mg

# 40. Vegan Cucumber and Bell Pepper Roll

This tasty Vegan Cucumber and Bell Pepper Roll adds a unique twist to a
classic veggie wrap. It is light and refreshing, and is a healthy and
delicious lunch or snack.
Serving:
Makes 4 rolls
Preparation time: 10 mins
Ready time: 10 mins

**Ingredients:**
-1 large cucumber
-1 red bell pepper
-1/4 cup vegan cream cheese
-1 tablespoon fresh minced dill
-2 tablespoons diced red onion
-1/4 teaspoon garlic powder
-Salt and black pepper to taste

**Instructions:**
1. Slice cucumber into 1/4 inch thick rounds.
2. Cut bell pepper into thick strips and cut into 4 even pieces.
3. Add cream cheese, dill, red onion, garlic powder, salt, and pepper in a
medium bowl. Stir to combine.
3. Place one cucumber round on a cutting board or plate. Spread one
teaspoon of cream cheese mixture onto the cucumber disc.
4. Place one piece of bell pepper on top of the cream cheese.
5. Start rolling the cucumber with the bell pepper until you've made a
tight roll.
6. Repeat for remaining cucumber and bell pepper.
7. Serve immediately.

**Nutrition information:**
Calories: 56 | Total Fat: 1.8 g | Sodium: 120 mg | Carbohydrates: 8.3 g
| Fiber: 1.2 g | Protein: 1.7 g

## 41. Vegan California Roll with Mango

Delight in this delicious vegan version of the classic California Roll with
an added tropical twist of mango! This easy-to-make roll is full of
nutritious Ingredients that are sure to please any palate.
Serving: Makes 4-6 rolls
Preparation time: 10 mins
Ready Time: 20 mins

**Ingredients:**
• 2 cups cooked sushi rice
• 4 sheets of seaweed
• 1 mango, cut into thin strips
• 1/2 avocado, sliced
• 1 cup cucumber, sliced
• 1/4 cup vegan mayo
• 2 tablespoons black sesame seeds

**Instructions:**
1. Cook sushi rice according to package instructions.
2. Cut mango, avocado, and cucumber into thin strips.
3. Place a sheet of seaweed on a sushi mat and spread 1/2 cup of sushi
rice over it.
4. Spread a thin layer of vegan mayo over the rice.
5. Layer the avocado, cucumber, and mango strips in the center of the
seaweed.
6. Wet the sides of the seaweed with a wet fingers and roll it up.
7. Use the mat neatly roll up the nori into a cylinder shape, squeezing it
together firmly as you go.
8. Sprinkle black sesame seeds over the rolls.
9. Repeat steps 3-8 until all of the Ingredients are used.
10. Slice the rolls and serve.

**Nutrition information: Per Serving (4-6 rolls): Calories: 151kcal, Carbohydrates: 27g, Protein: 3g, Fat: 5g, Saturated Fat: 1g, Sodium: 181 mg, Potassium: 239mg, Fiber: 4g, Sugar: 2g, Vitamin A: 315 IU, Vitamin C: 18mg, Calcium: 26mg, Iron: 1mg**

## 42. Vegan Teriyaki Jackfruit Roll

Vegan Teriyaki Jackfruit Roll is a delicious and creative vegan twist on sushi that is perfect for lunch or dinner.
Serving: 4
Preparation Time: 20 minutes
Ready Time: 30 minutes

**Ingredients:**
- 2 (20-ounce) cans young jackfruit, drained
- 1 tablespoon olive oil
- Salt, for taste
- 2 tablespoons soy sauce
- 1 tablespoon water
- 2 tablespoons maple syrup
- 2 teaspoons rice vinegar
- 2 tablespoons sesame oil
- 1 teaspoon grated ginger

**Instructions:**
1. Preheat the oven to 375°F.
2. Drain and rinse the jackfruit, then cut it into small cubes. Place jackfruit cubes onto a greased baking sheet, drizzle with olive oil, and sprinkle with salt.
3. Roast the jackfruit cubes for 10 minutes, then stir the cubes and bake for an additional 10 minutes.
4. Meanwhile, make the teriyaki sauce. In a small saucepan, heat soy sauce, water, and maple syrup over medium heat and bring to a simmer.
5. In a separate bowl, mix together rice vinegar, sesame oil, and grated ginger. Then add this mixture to the simmering saucepan and cook for 2 to 3 minutes.
6. Once jackfruit cubes are finished baking, add them to the teriyaki sauce and stir to combine. Simmer for an additional 5 minutes.

7. Serve jackfruit teriyaki in seaweed rolls and enjoy!

**Nutrition information:**
Per Serving: 180 calories, 8.2 g fat, 518 mg sodium, 13.1 g carbohydrates, 1.3 g dietary fiber, 8.2 g protein.

## 43. Vegan Tempura Shiitake Mushroom Roll

This vegan tempura shiitake mushroom roll is a delicious and nutritious way to get your servings of vegetables. It is crispy on the outside and tender on the inside, with a flavor-packed teriyaki sauce coating.
Serving: 4
Preparation time: 25 minutes
Ready time: 40 minutes

**Ingredients:**
- 1 lb shiitake mushrooms, cleaned and stems removed
- 2 cups all-purpose flour
- 4 cups vegetable oil for frying
- 1 teaspoon baking powder
- 1/2 teaspoon salt
- 2/3 cup cold water
- Teriyaki sauce for dipping

**Instructions:**
1. Preheat the vegetable oil in a deep-fryer or large, deep skillet to 375 degrees Fahrenheit.
2. Mix together the all-purpose flour, baking powder, and salt in a large bowl. Slowly stir in just enough cold water to make a thick batter.
3. Dip each shiitake mushroom into the batter, coating completely. Drop into the hot oil and fry for approximately 2 minutes, until golden brown.
4. Remove the tempura shiitake mushrooms from the oil to a paper towel-lined plate and let cool. Once cooled, arrange them in a row on a plate and roll up, tucking in any loose edges.
5. Serve with teriyaki sauce for dipping.

**Nutrition information:**

Calories: 141, Fat: 8 g, Saturated Fat: 1 g, Sodium: 120 mg,
Carbohydrates: 14 g, Fiber: 2 g, Protein: 5 g

## 44. Vegan Mango and Cucumber Roll

These vegan mango and cucumber rolls are the perfect combination of
sweet and crunchy. They are fun to make and make an excellent summer
appetizer or snack.
Serving: 4-5
Preparation Time: 10 minutes
Ready Time: 20 minutes

**Ingredients:**
- 2 ripe mangos, peeled and cut into cubes
- 1 medium cucumber, diced
- 1/4 cup of rolled oats
- 1 tablespoon of sesame seeds
- 1/8 cup of maple syrup
- 1 tablespoon of rice vinegar
- 2 tablespoons of olive oil
- Salt and pepper, to taste

**Instructions:**
1. Preheat oven to 350°F and line a baking sheet with parchment paper.
2. Place the mango cubes, cucumber cubes, and rolled oats on the baking
sheet.
3. Drizzle with maple syrup, rice vinegar, and olive oil.
4. Sprinkle with sesame seeds and season with salt and pepper.
5. Bake for 20 minutes, stirring occasionally, until lightly golden.
6. Remove from oven and let cool.
7. To serve, place a spoonful of the mango and cucumber mixture onto a
wrappable vegan wrap and roll up.

**Nutrition information: (per 1 wrap)**
Calories: 100
Fat: 4g
Carbohydrates: 16g
Protein: 2g

Fiber: 2g

## 45. Vegan Spicy Mayo and Avocado Roll

This vegan spicy mayo and avocado roll is a delicious and healthy treat that's easy to make. It has a sweet yet spicy flavor and creamy texture perfect for a quick snack, appetizer, or lunch.
Serving: 4
Preparation Time: 10 minutes
Ready Time: 20 minutes

**Ingredients:**
- 1/2 cup vegan mayonnaise
- 1 teaspoon chili garlic sauce
- 2 avocados, peeled and diced
- 2 tablespoons finely chopped red onion
- 4 nori sheets
- 1 tablespoon sesame seeds

**Instructions:**
1. In a small bowl, whisk together the vegan mayonnaise and chili garlic sauce.
2. In a separate bowl, mix the diced avocados, red onion, and sesame seeds.
3. On a flat work surface, lay out the nori sheets.
4. Evenly spread the vegan mayonnaise mixture over each sheet.
5. Sprinkle the avocado mixture over the mayonnaise.
6. Beginning with the end closest to you, start to roll the sheets as tightly as possible.
7. Use a sharp knife to slice the rolls into 1 inch pieces.
8. Serve immediately.

**Nutrition information: Per Serving: Calories: 220, Protein: 3 g, Total fat: 18 g, Saturated fat: 3 g, Cholesterol: 0 mg, Sodium: 190 mg, Carbohydrates: 11 g, Fiber: 5 g, Sugar: 1 g**

# 46. Vegan Peanut Tofu and Cucumber Roll

This simple vegan dish is a perfect snack or side dish for any meal. The tofu provides an interesting twist and great texture, while the cucumber and peanut butter provide crunch and sweetness.
Serving: 4
Preparation Time: 15 minutes
Ready Time: 15 minutes

**Ingredients:**
- 1 package of tofu, diced
- 1 cucumber, peeled and sliced
- 2 tablespoons peanut butter
- 2 tablespoons sesame oil
- 2 tablespoons soy sauce
- 2 cloves garlic, minced
- Salt and pepper, to taste

**Instructions:**
1. Heat a large skillet over medium-high heat. Add the diced tofu and cook until golden, stirring occasionally.
2. Add the cucumber slices and cook for an additional few minutes.
3. In a small bowl, whisk together the peanut butter, sesame oil, soy sauce, garlic, salt and pepper.
4. Pour the mixture over the tofu and cucumbers and stir to combine.
5. Cook for an additional few minutes until heated through.
6. Serve warm over rice or with your favorite side.

**Nutrition information: Per Serving: Calories 233, Fat 16g, Carbohydrates 10g, Protein 12g, Sodium 689mg, Cholesterol 0mg.**


# 47. Vegan Teriyaki Eggplant and Avocado Roll

This vegan teriyaki eggplant and avocado roll is a wonderful appetizer or side dish full of sweet and savory flavors that everyone will enjoy.
Serving: 2
Preparation time: 10 minutes
Ready time: 20 minutes

**Ingredients:**
- 1 eggplant, cut into slices
- 2 tbsp teriyaki sauce
- 2 avocados, peeled and sliced
- 2 small sheets of nori

**Instructions:**
1. Preheat oven to 200°C and line a baking sheet with parchment paper.
2. Arrange the eggplant slices on the lined baking sheet and brush each piece with 1/2 tbsp of teriyaki sauce.
3. Bake the eggplant for 15 minutes, or until lightly browned.
4. Lay one sheet of nori out on a plate, then top with baked eggplant slices and sliced avocado.
5. Roll the nori sheet tightly, using a sushi mat, and cut into bite-sized pieces.
6. Serve and enjoy!

**Nutrition information:**
1 serving (2 rolls) of this vegan teriyaki eggplant and avocado roll contains approx. 211 calories, 14g fat, 18g carbohydrates, and 5g protein.

## 48. Vegan Shiitake Mushroom and Radish Roll

Enjoy this delicious vegan shiitake mushroom and radish roll that is perfect for a light nutritous snack or lunch.
Serving: 4
Preparation time: 10 minutes
Ready time: 10 minutes

**Ingredients:**
-10 fresh shiitake mushrooms
-1 large radish
-1 garlic clove, grated
-2 tablespoons of olive oil
-2 tablespoons of tamari
-2 tablespoons of mirin
-2 teaspoons of sesame oil

-1 teaspoon of ginger, grated
-1 teaspoon of sugar
-4 sheets of nori

**Instructions:**
1. Start by prepping your vegetables. Thinly slice the shiitake mushrooms and radish.
2. In a mixing bowl, combine the mushrooms, radish, garlic, olive oil, tamari, mirin, sesame oil, ginger, and sugar. Mix everything together until evenly combined.
3. Next, lay out a sheet of nori on a clean surface and spread the mushroom and radish mixture on the bottom half of the nori.
4. Start rolling the nori from the bottom to the top, using your fingers to press the mixture together while rolling. Continue rolling until you've reached the top of the nori sheet.
5. Continue this process with the remaining filling and nori sheets.
6. When all your rolls are done, slice them into individual pieces.

**Nutrition information:**
Per Serving: Calories 130 | Total Fat 8 g | Saturated Fat 1 g | Cholesterol 0 mg | Sodium 280 mg | Total Carbohydrates 11 g | fiber 2 g | Sugar 6 g | Protein 3 g

## 49. Vegan Green Dragon Roll with Asparagus

This delicious Vegan Green Dragon Roll with Asparagus is an easy and flavourful vegan dinner recipe. Full of healthy, vibrant veggies, it's the perfect way to add a tasty and healthy meal to your menu.
Serving: Serves 4
Preparation time: 10 minutes
Ready Time: 30 minutes

**Ingredients:**
- 2 cups cooked sushi rice
- 1 teaspoon light soy sauce
- 2 tablespoons nutritional yeast
- 2 tablespoons freshly squeezed lemon juice
- 4 sheets nori seaweed

- 4 carrots, cut into thin matchsticks
- 1 red pepper, cut into thin matchsticks
- 1 cucumber, cut into thin matchsticks
- 1 bunch asparagus, cut into thin matchsticks
- 2 tablespoons sesame seeds, for garnish
- Pickled ginger and wasabi, for Serving:

**Instructions:**
1. In a large bowl, combine cooked sushi rice, soy sauce, nutritional yeast, and lemon juice and mix well.
2. On each nori sheet, place 1/4 of the mixed vegetables, forming them into a rectangular shape.
3. Place equal amounts of the rice mixture on top of the vegetables, pressing it down so it sticks together.
4. Roll up each nori sheet, tucking the ends in and rolling it away from you. Slice each roll into 8 pieces with a sharp knife.
5. Garnish each roll with sesame seeds and serve with pickled ginger and wasabi.

**Nutrition information**
Calories: 158, Protein: 4.3g, Total Fat: 2.7g, Saturated Fat 0.7g, Carbohydrates: 28.3g, Sodium: 181.1mg, Fiber: 3.2g, Sugar: 5.8g

## 50. Vegan Spicy Vegetable and Avocado Roll

This delicious and healthy vegan roll is an easy and tasty way to get your daily dose of vegetables! It's filled with spicy vegetables such as bell peppers, onions, mushrooms, and jalapeños, and then topped with a creamy avocado spread to balance out the flavors.
Serving: Makes 4 rolls
Preparation time: 15 minutes
Ready time: 30 minutes

**Ingredients:**
- 4 sheets of nori seaweed
- 1/2 bell pepper, diced
- 1/4 onion, diced
- 1/4 cup mushrooms, diced

- 1/4 cup jalapeños, diced
- 1 tablespoon olive oil
- 1/2 teaspoon garlic powder
- 1/2 teaspoon cayenne pepper
- 1/4 teaspoon paprika
- 1/2 cup cooked brown rice
- 1 avocado, mashed

**Instructions:**
1. Preheat the oven to 375 degrees F.
2. Heat olive oil in a skillet over medium heat. Add bell peppers, onion, mushrooms, and jalapeños and sauté until the vegetables are softened, about 5 minutes.
3. Add garlic powder, cayenne pepper, and paprika and cook for 1 more minute.
4. Remove from heat, and combine cooked vegetables with the cooked brown rice.
5. Lay a sheet of nori out on a flat surface and spread a thin layer of the avocado mash onto the nori.
6. Place 1/4 of the vegetable mixture onto the avocado and gently roll up the nori.
7. Place the roll onto a parchment-lined baking sheet and repeat with the other 3 sheets of nori.
8. Bake in the preheated oven for 10 minutes.
9. Slice the rolls into 3 pieces and serve with extra avocado mash, if desired.

**Nutrition information:**
Calories: 141, Total Fat: 7.2g, Cholesterol: 0mg, Sodium: 11.7mg, Carbohydrates: 17g, Protein: 3.1g, Fiber: 4.9g.

## 51. Vegan Tempura Avocado and Cucumber Roll

Enjoy the crispiness of tempura in this vegan version that features sliced cucumber and avocado rolled in seaweed. This is a great meal option for vegans and vegetarians.
Serving: 4
Preparation time: 20 minutes

Ready time: 20 minutes

**Ingredients:**
- 2 cup tempura coating mix
- ¾ cup water
- 1 cucumber, thinly sliced
- 2 ripe avocados, cut into strips
- 4 sheets of nori (seaweed sheets)
- 2 tablespoons sesame oil
- 2 tablespoons soy sauce

**Instructions:**
1. In a shallow bowl, mix the tempura coating mix and water together until it forms a thin batter.
2. Dip the cucumber slices and avocado strips into the batter and coat them evenly.
3. Lay a sheet of nori on a flat surface and place the tempura-coated cucumber and avocado strips in the center.
4. Roll the nori sheet up tightly, securing the edges with a little water if needed.
5. Heat the sesame oil in a large skillet over medium-high heat.
6. Place the rolled sushi on the skillet and let it cook for about 3-4 minutes, flipping it occasionally until it is golden brown.
7. Serve with soy sauce.

**Nutrition information:**
Calories - 285
Total Fat - 17.2g
Saturated Fat - 2.5g
Cholesterol - 0mg
Sodium - 780.9mg
Total Carb - 26.7g
Dietary Fiber - 9.3g
Sugars - 4.3g
Protein - 6g

## 52. Vegan Mango and Sweet Potato Roll

This vegan mango and sweet potato roll is a delicious combination of flavors that will make you plan your next dinner.
Serving: 4
Preparation time: 25 minutes
Ready time: 45 minutes

**Ingredients:**
- 1 mango, thinly sliced
- 1 large sweet potato, peeled and diced
- 2 tablespoons olive oil
- 1 teaspoon garlic powder
- 2 tablespoons nutritional yeast
- 1 teaspoon sea salt
- 1 teaspoon black pepper

**Instructions:**
1. Preheat the oven to 375 degrees.
2. In a mixing bowl, combine the diced sweet potato with olive oil, garlic powder, nutritional yeast, salt, and pepper. Toss to coat.
3. Spread the sweet potato mixture onto a baking sheet lined with parchment paper and bake for 30 minutes.
4. Peel mango and thinly slice.
5. Once the sweet potato is finished cooking, let cool.
6. Place sweet potato and mango slices on a serving platter and roll or fold them together.

**Nutrition information:**
Serving size: 1 roll
Calories: 77 kcal
Fat: 4.5g
Carbohydrates: 10.2g
Protein: 1g
Fiber: 1.5g

## 53. Vegan Philadelphia Roll with Carrot Lox

This vegan version of the classic Philadelphia roll is packed with flavor and texture and requires just a few simple Ingredients. It features a creamy avocado base, vegan carrot lox, and cucumber for a little crunch.
Serving: 4-5 rolls
Preparation time: 20 minutes
Ready time: 20 minutes

**Ingredients:**
- Nori sheets
- 1 ripe avocado
- 2 carrots
- 2 tablespoons tamari
- 1 tablespoon mirin
- 2 tablespoons olive oil
- ⅓ cup vegan mayo
- 1 cucumber

**Instructions:**
1. Preheat oven to 400 degrees F (200 C).
2. Thinly slice the carrots and marinate them in tamari and mirin for 15 minutes.
3. Line a baking sheet with foil and spread the carrots in an even layer. Bake in the preheated oven for 20-25 minutes, until golden and crisp.
4. Meanwhile, mash the avocado in a small bowl.
5. Slice the cucumber into thin strips.
6. Spread the avocado mixture onto each nori sheet, leaving a gap at one end.
7. Top with the cucumber strips and carrot lox.
8. Starting from the end with the gap, roll the nori sheets up into tight cylinders.
9. Slice each roll into 5 pieces and serve with the vegan mayo.

**Nutrition information (per serving):**
Calories: 194
Fat: 16g
Carbohydrates: 12g
Protein: 3g
Fiber: 5g

# 54. Vegan Peanut Avocado and Cucumber Roll

This vegan-friendly sushi roll combines the natural flavors of avocado, cucumber, and peanut for a delicious, crunchy, and healthy meal.
Serving: Makes 6 rolls
Preparation Time: 10 minutes
Ready Time: 20 minutes

**Ingredients:**
- 1 ripe avocado, thinly sliced
- 1 large cucumber, thinly sliced
- 6 sheets of nori
- ⅓ cup of crushed peanuts
- 1 to 2 tablespoons of sesame oil
- 2 tablespoons of agave syrup
- 2 tablespoons of rice vinegar
- Pinch of sea salt
- Cooked sushi rice

**Instructions:**
1. Begin by preparing the sliced avocado and cucumber and set aside.
2. Lay out a sheet of nori onto a clean and dry surface.
3. Spread a thin layer of cooked sushi rice onto the nori sheet and leave the top ⅓ of the sheet void of rice.
4. Then, evenly spread a generous layer of crushed peanuts onto the rice.
5. On the top ⅓ of the sheet of nori, arrange the sliced avocado and cucumbers onto the sheet, creating a row of toppings.
6. Drizzle a thin layer of sesame oil, agave syrup, and rice vinegar over the toppings.
7. Use a rolling mat or your hand to roll the sushi, beginning from the end with the toppings.
8. Roll until the end of the sheet, press lightly to seal and cut the roll into six equal pieces.
9. Repeat with the remaining sheets of nori and Ingredients.

**Nutrition information:**
Serving Size: 1 roll
Calories: 145
Carbohydrates: 21g

Protein: 4g
Fat: 6g
Saturated Fat: 1g
Sugar: 4g
Sodium: 201mg
Fiber: 2g

## 55. Vegan Spicy Tofu Tempura and Asparagus Roll

This delicious vegan wrap is a unique combination of spicy tofu tempura
and crunchy asparagus rolled in a wrap to create a perfect Asian-inspired
treat.
Serving: 3
Preparation time: 25 minutes
Ready time: 25 minutes

**Ingredients:**
- 2 cups of tofu, cubed
- 1 cup all-purpose flour
- 2 teaspoon chili powder
- 1 teaspoon garlic powder
- Salt and pepper to taste
- 1/2 cup vegetable oil
- 2 tablespoons sriracha sauce
- 2 tablespoons soy sauce
- 1 tablespoon rice vinegar
- 6 Asparagus, washed and trimmed
- 2 Large wraps

**Instructions:**
1. In a large bowl, mix together the tofu cubes, flour, chili powder, garlic
powder, salt and pepper.
2. Heat oil in a large skillet over medium-high heat.
3. When the oil is hot, add the coated tofu cubes, stirring occasionally
until golden brown and crisp.
4. In a separate bowl, mix together the sriracha sauce, soy sauce and rice
vinegar.
5. Add the asparagus to the skillet and cook until tender.

6. Place the cooked tofu and asparagus in the wrap, then sprinkle with sauce.
7. Roll up the wrap and enjoy.

**Nutrition information: (per serving)**
Calories: 330
Fat: 19g
Protein: 14g
Carbohydrates: 24g
Fiber: 4g
Sugars: 2g

# 56. Vegan Crunchy Spicy Mayo and Shiitake Mushroom Roll

This vegan crunchy spicy mayo and shiitake mushroom roll is a unique and delicious Japanese-inspired vegan dish. It is crunchy on the outside, creamy and spicy on the inside, and full of flavor.
Serving: 2
Preparation time: 20 minutes
Ready time: 45 minutes

**Ingredients:**
- 10 shiitake mushrooms
- 2 tablespoons vegan mayonnaise
- 1 tablespoon sriracha
- 2 tablespoons sesame oil
- 1/2 teaspoon sesame seeds
- 2 sheets nori
- 4 cups cooked short-grain sushi rice
- 2 tablespoons tamari

**Instructions:**
1. Preheat oven to 400°F.
2. Place mushrooms on a baking sheet and bake in preheated oven for 10 minutes.
3. In a small bowl, combine mayonnaise, sriracha, sesame oil, and sesame seeds.

4. Cut the nori into four 5-inch squares.
5. Divide the cooked sushi rice into four portions.
6. To assemble the rolls, place a square of nori on a rolling mat, spoon 1/4 of the sushi rice onto the nori and spread evenly, leaving a 1-inch border at the top.
7. Place the cooked mushrooms in the center of the rice.
8. Drizzle 1/4 of the mayo mixture over the mushrooms.
9. Starting with the bottom edge, slowly roll the nori up, making sure to keep the edges sealed.
10. Using a very sharp knife, slice the roll into 4 equal pieces.
11. Serve the rolls with tamari for dipping.

**Nutrition information:**
Calories: 340
Protein: 7.9g
Carbs: 55.9g
Fiber: 2.8g
Fat: 9.3g

## 57. Vegan Teriyaki Portobello and Cucumber Roll

This vegan teriyaki portobello and cucumber roll is a flavorful, nourishing dish that is perfect for a light and healthy lunch. With vegan friendly Ingredients like mushrooms and cucumbers, this easy and delicious recipe can be made in only a few steps.
Serving: 2
Preparation Time: 10 minutes
Ready Time: 15 minutes

**Ingredients:**
• 2 large portobello mushrooms
• ¼ cup teriyaki sauce
• 2 Persian cucumbers
• 1 teaspoon sesame oil
• 2 tablespoons white sesame seeds
• 2 sheets nori, cut in half

**Instructions:**

1. Preheat the oven to 375°F and coat the mushrooms with 1 tablespoon of teriyaki sauce. Place them on a baking sheet and bake for 10 minutes.
2. Meanwhile, cut the cucumbers into thin strips and combine with the sesame oil and the remaining teriyaki sauce.
3. When the mushrooms are done, remove from oven and let cool before assembling the rolls.
4. Place a nori sheet on a cutting board. Spread out the cucumber mixture and top with some sesame seeds.
5. Place the mushrooms in the middle and roll up tightly. Cut into pieces and serve.

**Nutrition information:**
• Calories: 287
• Total Fat: 13g
• Cholesterol: 0mg
• Sodium: 837mg
• Total Carbohydrate: 22g
• Dietary Fiber: 5g
• Protein: 15g

## 58. Vegan Tempura Asparagus and Avocado Roll

Vegetarian Tempura Asparagus and Avocado Roll is a nutritious and tasty dish loaded with protein, fiber, and minerals. Enjoy the crunchy texture of the tempura with the flavors of the asparagus and avocado for a flavorful meal.
Serving: 4
Preparation Time: 10 minutes
Ready Time: 15 minutes

**Ingredients:**
• 1 bunch asparagus
• 2 avocados, pitted and sliced
• 1 tablespoon all-purpose flour
• 1/2 teaspoon baking powder
• 1/2 teaspoon sugar
• 1/4 teaspoon salt
• 1/2 cup plus 2 tablespoons cold water

• 1/2 cup canola oil for frying

**Instructions:**
1. Heat oil in a deep pan or pot over medium-high heat.
2. Whisk together the flour, baking powder, sugar, and salt in a medium bowl. Slowly whisk in the cold water until the mixture is smooth.
3. Dip each asparagus spear into the batter and carefully add to the hot oil. Fry in batches for about 3 minutes or until golden brown. Remove with a slotted spoon and place onto a paper towel-lined plate.
4. Lay out 4 pieces of nori wrap. Place 4 spears of asparagus horizontally in the center, and add avocado slices in the center.
5. Wet the outside edge of the nori wrap and roll it up. Slice with a sharp knife and serve.

**Nutrition information:**
Per serving:  440 calories; 18.3 g fat; 51.5 g carbohydrates; 7.1 g protein; 9.5 g fiber; 530 mg sodium.

## 59. Vegan Mango and Jalapeno Roll with Radish

Try this vegan mango and jalapeno roll with radish - a refreshing and tantalizing dish sure to leave you feeling satisfied!
Serving: 4 rolls
Preparation Time: 10 minutes
Ready Time: 20 minutes

**Ingredients:**
- 4 rice paper wrappers
- 2 mangoes, diced
- 1 jalapeno, finely diced
- 1/4 cup fresh radish, shredded
- 1/4 cup coriander leaves, chopped

**Instructions:**
1. Soak a rice paper wrapper in lukewarm water for 5-10 seconds. Place on a plate.
2. Distribute the diced mango, jalapeno, radish, and coriander leaves on the rice paper wrapper.

3. Carefully wrap the wrapper up, tucking in the sides.
4. Repeat the process with the remaining wrappers and filling.
5. Serve the rolls with desired accompaniments.

**Nutrition information:**
Per Serving (1 roll): Calories: 88, Total Fat: 0g, Cholesterol: 0mg,
Sodium: 18mg, Carbohydrates: 22g, Dietary Fiber: 2g, Sugars: 9g,
Protein: 1g

## 60. Vegan BBQ Mushroom and Cucumber Roll

This simple and delicious vegan recipe for BBQ Mushroom and
Cucumber Rolls will be a hit at your next gathering! The recipe is easy to
make and requires only a few simple Ingredients.
Serving: Makes 4 rolls
Preparation time: 5 minutes
Ready time: 25 minutes

**Ingredients:**
- 4 sheets of prepared sushi seaweed
- 10 oz oyster mushrooms, sliced
- 2 tablespoons vegetable oil
- 1 teaspoon of garlic powder
- 1 teaspoon of onion powder
- 2 tablespoons of maple syrup
- 2 tablespoons of soy sauce
- 2 cucumbers, sliced lengthwise
- Salt, black pepper
- 4 tablespoons of vegan mayonnaise

**Instructions:**
1. Preheat the oven to 400°F.
2. In a bowl, combine the mushrooms, oil, garlic powder, onion powder,
maple syrup, and soy sauce. Mix with a spoon until the mushrooms are
fully coated.
3. Place the mixture on a greased baking sheet and bake for 15 minutes.
4. Place the cucumber slices on a plate lined with a paper towel and
season with salt and pepper.

5. Place a sheet of seaweed on a flat surface. Spread the vegan mayonnaise evenly over the sheet.
6. Place the roasted mushrooms on the seaweed. Arrange the cucumber slices on top.
7. Roll the seaweed, being careful not to tear it. Slice the roll into 4 equal pieces.

**Nutrition information: Calories: 210; Total Fat: 7g; Sodium: 450mg; Carbohydrates: 28g; Fiber: 5g; Protein: 7g**

# 61. Avocado and Radish Roll with Carrot Lox

This delicious vegan appetizer is a great way to add flavor and texture to your meals. Featuring carrots, avocados, radishes, and a delicious lemon cream cheese spread, it can be served hot or cold, and makes an excellent addition to any meal.
Serving: Serves 4-6
Preparation time: 10 minutes
Ready time: 20 minutes

**Ingredients:**
- 2 carrots, peeled and thinly sliced
- 2 avocado, mashed
- 2 radishes, sliced
- 2 tablespoons of cream cheese
- 2 tablespoons of lemon juice
- Salt and pepper, to taste

**Instructions:**
1. Preheat oven to 375 F.
2. Cut the carrots and radishes into thin slices.
3. In a bowl, mash the avocado and mix in the cream cheese, lemon juice, salt, and pepper.
4. On a cutting board, place the carrot slices in overlapping circles.
5. Spread the mashed avocado mixture on top of the carrots and top with the radish slices.
6. Working from the outside in, roll up the carrot slices with the avocado and radish to make a roll.

7. Place the roll onto a greased baking sheet and bake in the preheated oven for 15-20 minutes, until golden brown.
8. Serve with your favorite dip!

**Nutrition information: Per serving – Calories: 133; Carbohydrates: 12g; Sugars: 2g; Cholesterol: 0mg; Fiber: 3g; Protein: 2g; Fat: 8g.**

## 62. Vegan Dynamite Spicy Mayo and Sweet Potato Roll

This Vegan Dynamite Spicy Mayo and Sweet Potato Roll is a healthy, flavorful dish that's sure to please your taste buds. The combination of sweet potato, vegan mayonnaise, and spices gives this roll a unique and spicy flavor. It's a great addition to any meal.
Serving: Makes 8 rolls.
Preparation time: 10 minutes
Ready time: 25 minutes

**Ingredients:**
- 1/2 cup vegan mayonnaise
- 2 tablespoons sriracha sauce
- 2 tablespoons minced green onion
- 2 teaspoons minced garlic
- 1/2 teaspoon black pepper
- 8 ounces vegan cheese
- 4 large sweet potatoes, cut into thin slices

**Instructions:**
1. Preheat oven to 350°F.
2. In a small bowl, mix together vegan mayonnaise, sriracha, green onion, garlic and black pepper.
3. Line a baking sheet with parchment paper and arrange the sweet potato slices in one layer.
4. Spread the mayonnaise mixture on the sweet potato slices.
5. Top with vegan cheese.
6. Bake in the preheated oven for 20-25 minutes or until cheese is melted and edges of sweet potatoes are lightly browned.
7. Serve warm.

**Nutrition information:**
One roll contains 189 calories, 11g fat, 9.5g carbohydrates, 8g protein.

## 63. Vegan Teriyaki Tofu and Bell Pepper Roll

This flavorful vegan teriyaki tofu and bell pepper roll is the perfect dish for a light lunch or dinner. With all the delicious flavor of teriyaki sauce and the added crunch of bell pepper and fried tofu, this roll will be sure to satisfy.
Serving: 2
Preparation Time: 20 minutes
Ready Time: 15 minutes

**Ingredients:**
- 1 package fried tofu, cubed
- 2 bell peppers, julienned
- 2 tablespoons teriyaki sauce
- ½ teaspoon ground ginger
- Salt to taste
- Peanut oil for sautéing

**Instructions:**
1. Heat 2 tablespoons of peanut oil in a large skillet over medium-high heat.
2. Add the cubed tofu and sauté for 5 minutes.
3. Add the bell peppers to the skillet and stir.
4. Reduce heat to low and add the teriyaki sauce, ground ginger, and salt.
5. Simmer for 5 minutes.
6. Place the mixture in the center of a sheet of nori and roll it up into a cylinder.
7. Place roll in the refrigerator to cool and set for 10 minutes.

**Nutrition information: (per serving)**
Calories: 256 kCal
Fat: 9.3g
Carbohydrates: 12.6g
Protein: 15.2g

# 64. Vegan Shiitake Mushroom and Avocado Roll with Radish

Enjoy this delicious vegan sushi roll that combines the umami flavor of shiitake mushrooms with the creamy texture of avocado and the crunch of radish all sandwiched between two layers of nori.
Serving: 4
Preparation Time: 15 minutes
Ready Time: 15 minutes

**Ingredients:**
- 4 sheets of nori
- 4 tablespoons vegan sushi rice
- 4 tablespoons diced radish
- 8 shiitake mushrooms, sliced
- 1 avocado, sliced
- Soy sauce or ponzu sauce, for dipping

**Instructions:**
1. Place a sheet of nori on a sushi rolling mat.
2. Pat a thin layer of vegan sushi rice onto the nori.
3. Layer the radish, mushrooms, and avocado on the nori.
4. Starting from the edge closest to you, roll the nori away from you to form a cylinder.
5. Repeat for each roll.
6. Cut each roll into 8 pieces using a sharp knife.
7. Serve with soy sauce or ponzu sauce for dipping.

**Nutrition information:**
Each Vegan Shiitake Mushroom and Avocado Roll contains approximately 130 calories, 4g protein, 5g fat, and 18g carbohydrates.

# 65. Vegan Spicy Peanut and Cucumber Roll

Vegan Spicy Peanut and Cucumber Roll is a unique version of a peanut wrap filled with flavorful Ingredients. This vegan wrap tastes and looks like an amazing appetizer that will have everyone asking for more.
Serving: Makes 4-6 wraps.
Preparation time: 25 minutes
Ready time: 25 minutes

**Ingredients:**
 4-6 whole wheat tortillas, 1/4 cup vegan peanut butter, 2 tablespoons hot sauce, 1/4 teaspoon garlic powder, 1 large cucumber, sliced into thin sticks, 1/4 cup vegan sour cream

**Instructions:**
  1. Preheat oven to 350°F.
2. Spread entire tortilla with peanut butter.
3. Mix together hot sauce, garlic powder, and vegan sour cream.
4. Spread the mixture evenly over the peanut butter.
5. Place the cucumber sticks in the center of the tortilla.
6. Roll the tortilla tightly and place onto baking sheet.
7. Bake for 8 minutes, or until lightly golden.
8. Slice each wrap into thirds before serving.

**Nutrition information: Calories: 220, Carbs: 28 g, Protein: 9 g, Fat: 8 g**

## 66. Vegan Cucumber and Bell Pepper Roll with Carrot Lox

An easy vegan cucumber roll filled with bell peppers and carrot lox. Serves as an ideal snack or light meal with a refreshingly light and deliciously savory flavor.
Serving: 2 rolls
Preparation Time: 10 mins
Ready Time: 15 mins

**Ingredients:**
- 2 cucumbers
- ½ bell pepper

- 2-3 oz vegan cream cheese
- 2 tablespoons vegan mayonnaise
- 1 teaspoon dried dill
- 1 large carrot
- 2 tablespoons olive oil
- 1 teaspoon salt

**Instructions:**
1. Peel and thinly slice the carrot into thin strips.
2. Heat olive oil in a pan over medium heat. Add the carrot strips and cook for about 5 minutes, stirring often.
3. In a medium bowl, combine mayo, cream cheese, dill, and ½ teaspoon of salt. Mix together until fully blended.
4. Slice the cucumber into thin lengthwise strips.
5. Cut the bell pepper into thin strips.
6. Spread some of the cream cheese mixture onto each cucumber strip.
7. Top the cream cheese spread with some of the bell pepper and carrot strips.
8. Roll up the cucumber strips, starting from one end to the other.
9. Serve and enjoy!

**Nutrition information:**
Calories: 153 kcal, Carbohydrates: 8.4 g, Protein: 3.1 g, Fat: 11.8 g, Saturated Fat: 4.2 g, Sodium: 444 mg, Fiber: 2.3 g, Sugar: 4.6 g

## 67. Vegan California Roll with Mango and Avocado

This vegan version of the classic California roll features the iconic nori wrap filled with cucumber, avocado, and mango for a delightfully bright and flavorful ingredient combination.
Serving: Makes 4 rolls
Preparation Time: 10 minutes
Ready Time: 15 minutes

**Ingredients:**
- 4 sheets of nori
- 1 mango, diced
- 1 avocado, diced

- 1 cucumber, diced
- 2 cups cooked sushi rice

**Instructions:**
1. Spread 1 sheet of nori on a flat surface, shiny-side down.
2. Wet your hands with a bit of water and spread 1/4 of the sushi rice onto the nori.
3. Sprinkle one fourth of the diced mango, avocado, and cucumber across the top. Make sure to spread it out evenly.
4. Starting from the top, roll the nori away from you, using your fingers to keep the roll tight.
5. Cut the roll into 8 equal pieces.
6. Repeat steps 1-5 to prepare 3 more rolls.

**Nutrition information:**
Calories: 43 kcal, Carbohydrates: 10 g, Protein: 1 g, Fat: 1 g, Saturated Fat: 0.2 g, Sodium: 3 mg, Potassium: 181 mg, Fiber: 2.3 g, Sugar: 2.9 g, Vitamin A: 578 IU, Vitamin C: 14 mg, Calcium: 13 mg, Iron: 1 mg

# 68. Vegan Teriyaki Jackfruit and Asparagus Roll

This vegan teriyaki jackfruit and asparagus roll is a delicious and nutritious meal. It is packed with flavor and is low in fat and calories.
Serving: 2
Preparation Time: 25 minutes
Ready Time: 1-2 hours (for marinating)

**Ingredients:**
• 2 cans of jackfruit
• 1 bunch of asparagus
• 2 tablespoons of fresh grated ginger
• 4 tablespoons of tamari or soy sauce
• 2 tablespoons of brown sugar
• 2 tablespoons of rice vinegar
• 2 tablespoons of sesame oil
• Salt and pepper to taste

**Instructions:**

1. Drain and rinse the jackfruit and cut into thin strips.
2. Thinly slice the asparagus.
3. In a medium-sized bowl, whisk together the ginger, tamari, brown sugar, rice vinegar, sesame oil, salt, and pepper.
4. Add the jackfruit and asparagus to the bowl and mix to combine.
5. Marinate in the refrigerator for 1-2 hours.
6. Preheat the oven to 350°F.
7. Line a baking sheet with parchment paper.
8. Arrange the marinated jackfruit and asparagus onto the parchment paper.
9. Bake for 25 minutes or until the vegetables are tender and lightly browned.
10. Serve with your favorite accompaniments.

**Nutrition information: (Per Serving)**
Calories: 112, Total Fat: 2g, Saturated Fat: 0g, Cholesterol: 0mg, Sodium: 942mg, Carbohydrates: 20g, Dietary Fiber: 6g, Sugars: 10g, Protein: 3g.

## 69. Vegan Tempura Shiitake Mushroom and Cucumber Roll

A classic vegan sushi roll, this Vegan Tempura Shiitake Mushroom and Cucumber Roll is a great option for those looking for a delicious, vegetarian meal.
Serving: 4
Preparation Time: 45 minutes
Ready Time: 1 hour

**Ingredients:**
• 8 shiitake mushrooms
• Tempura batter
• 4 tsp vegetable oil
• 200g cooked sushi rice
• 120g cucumber ribbons
• 2 tbsp black or white sesame seeds
• 4 nori sheets, cut into 6-by-9-inch pieces

**Instructions:**

1. Preheat the oven to 190°C (375°F).
2. Slice the mushrooms lengthwise to make thin slices.
3. Make a tempura batter according to package directions.
4. Heat the vegetable oil in a frying pan over a medium heat.
5. Dip the mushroom slices into the tempura batter and fry them for 1 minute or until golden.
6. Place the fried mushrooms on a baking tray lined with baking paper and bake in the preheated oven for 8 minutes.
7. Place the cooked sushi rice onto a flat work surface and spread it out evenly.
8. Place a sheet of nori onto the rice.
9. Arrange the cucumber ribbons and fried mushrooms onto the nori facing inwards.
10. Sprinkle the sesame seeds over the vegetables.
11. Roll up the nori sheet from the bottom.
12. Cut the roll into 8 pieces.

**Nutrition information: Per serving: 126 calories, 7g of protein, 16g carbohydrate, 4g fat (1g saturated fat), 7g fibre, 17mg sodium.**

## 70. Vegan Mango and Cucumber Roll with Radish

Treat your taste buds to this delicious yet nutritious vegan mango and cucumber roll with radish! Not only is it packed with flavor but it's also filled with vitamins and minerals that are good for you.
Serving: 4
Preparation Time: 20 minutes
Ready Time: 20 minutes

**Ingredients:**
- 2 mangoes, peeled and cut into matchsticks
- 1 cucumber, peeled and cut into matchsticks
- 2 radishes, peeled and cut into matchsticks
- 4 sheets of nori seaweed
- 2 tablespoons of agave syrup
- 2 tablespoons of sesame oil
- 1 teaspoon of black sesame seeds

**Instructions:**
1. Preheat oven to 200°C (400°F).
2. Place matchstick pieces of mango, cucumber and radish in a bowl.
3. Drizzle agave syrup and sesame oil over mixture and mix together.
4. Place a sheet of nori seaweed on a baking sheet.
5. Spread matchstick mixture onto nori seaweed sheet.
6. Sprinkle black sesame seeds over the mixture.
7. Roll up nori seaweed sheet from one end to make a roll.
8. Repeat steps 4-7 with remaining nori seaweed sheets.
9. Bake in oven for 10-15 minutes, or until the nori seaweed is crispy.
10. Cut into pieces and serve.

**Nutrition information: Calories: 227; Fat: 5.3g; Carbs: 38g; Protein: 2.2g; Fiber: 5.5g; Sugar: 23.3g**


## 71. Vegan Spicy Mayo and Avocado Roll with Carrot Lox

This tasty vegan dish is a take on the classic sushi roll, bursting with flavor from vegan carrot lox and spicy mayo. It's easy to make and will be ready for you to enjoy in no time at all!
Serving: 2
Preparation time: 20 minutes
Ready time: 20 minutes

**Ingredients:**
- 2 sheets of vegan nori seaweed
- 1 medium avocado
- 2 tablespoons plant-based mayonnaise
- 1 tablespoon Sriracha
- 1 cup grated carrots
- 1 teaspoon liquid smoke
- 1 tablespoon lemon juice
- Salt and pepper to taste
- 1 tablespoon sesame oil
- 1 teaspoon maple syrup

**Instructions:**

1. Preheat the oven to 350°F.
2. In a bowl, combine the grated carrots, liquid smoke, lemon juice, salt, and pepper. Spread evenly onto a baking sheet lined with parchment paper.
3. Bake for 10 minutes, remove and let cool.
4. In a separate bowl, combine the mayonnaise, Sriracha, sesame oil, and maple syrup.
5. Place one sheet of nori onto a cutting board and spread half of the spicy mayo mixture onto one side.
6. Place half of the avocado slices in a horizontal line and half of the cooled carrot lox in the same line on top of the avocado.
7. Roll the nori into a circle and cut into 8 pieces.
8. Repeat with the remaining Ingredients and serve.

**Nutrition information (per serving): Calories: 158, Fat: 10g, Saturated Fat: 1.5g, Sugar: 5g, Sodium: 280mg**

## 72. Vegan Peanut Tofu and Bell Pepper Roll with Carrot Lox

Healthy and delicious, this vegan-friendly meal packs a punch for your tastebuds! With creamy peanut tofu, crunchy veggies, and a carrot lox topping, this vegan recipe is sure to please.
Serving: 2-3
Preparation Time: 25 minutes
Ready Time: 45 minutes

**Ingredients:**
- 1 package extra firm tofu
- 2 bell peppers (sliced)
- 2 tablespoons peanut butter
- 2 tablespoons tamari or soy sauce
- 2 tablespoons sesame oil
- 2 tablespoons chilli paste
- 2 cloves garlic (minced)
- 1 teaspoon ground ginger
- 1 teaspoon sriracha
- 2 tablespoons olive oil

- 2 carrots (shredded)
- 1 tablespoon liquid smoke

**Instructions:**
1. Preheat the oven to 400F (200C).
2. Remove the tofu from the package and press it between paper towels to drain as much moisture as possible.
3. Cut the tofu into strips and place them onto a parchment paper-lined baking sheet.
4. In a small bowl, whisk together the peanut butter, tamari, sesame oil, chili paste, garlic, ginger, and sriracha.
5. Brush the mixture over the tofu pieces and bake for 20 minutes, flipping once halfway through.
6. While the tofu is baking, prepare the bell peppers. Heat the olive oil in a pan over medium heat.
7. Add the bell peppers and sauté for 5-7 minutes until softened.
8. In a separate bowl, mix together the shredded carrots, liquid smoke, and 2 tablespoons of water.
9. When the tofu is done baking, assemble the rolls. Place one piece of tofu onto a plate and spread it with the carrot mixture.
10. Place a few pieces of bell peppers on top and roll it up. Serve immediately.

**Nutrition information: Per Serving (3 servings): Calories: 255 kcal, Protein: 14 g, Carbohydrates: 12 g, Fat: 18 g, Saturated Fat: 3 g, Sodium: 800 mg, Fiber: 3 g, Sugar: 5 g, Vitamin A: 684 IU, Vitamin C: 54 mg, Calcium: 55 mg, Iron: 1.6 mg**

## 73. Vegan Teriyaki Eggplant and Avocado Roll with Radish

This flavorful vegan dish combines the sweet and savory taste of teriyaki with the crunch of radish and the creaminess of avocado in a vivid sushi-style roll. This quick and easy-to-make meal is sure to become a favorite vegan staple.
Serving: 5
Preparation Time: 10 minutes
Ready Time: 20 minutes

**Ingredients:**
1/3 cup teriyaki sauce
1/2 cup cooked eggplant
1/2 cup radishes, finely chopped
1 avocado, cubed
Sushi rice, cooked and cooled

**Instructions:**
1. In a small bowl, whisk together teriyaki sauce with 1 tablespoon of warm water.
2. Place eggplant on a cutting board, and cut into thin strips. Toss eggplant strips in the teriyaki sauce.
3. On a sheet of nori seaweed, spread cooled sushi rice. Place strips of eggplant, radish, and avocado on top of the nori.
4. Roll up the nori, using a bamboo rolling mat, and cut into pieces.
5. Serve rolls with remaining teriyaki sauce.

**Nutrition information:**
Calories: 219, Protein: 8g, Fat: 9g, Fiber: 7g, Carbohydrates: 27g, Sugar: 7g

## 74. Vegan Shiitake Mushroom and Radish Roll with Carrot Lox

Enjoy a vegan take on classic smoked salmon and cream cheese bagel with this Shiitake Mushroom and Radish Roll with Carrot Lox. This delicious and savory recipe uses shiitake mushrooms and radishes to create a flavorful and vegan-friendly alternative to the traditional salmon option.
Serving: Makes 8 rolls
Preparation time: 15 minutes
Ready time: 40 minutes

**Ingredients:**
• ½ cup shiitake mushrooms, diced
• ¼ cup radish, small dice
• 2 tablespoons dill, finely chopped

• 2 tablespoons vegan cream cheese
• 2 cups carrot lox, thinly sliced
• 4 large wraps or tortillas

**Instructions:**
1. Preheat oven to 375°F.
2. In a medium bowl, mix together shiitake mushrooms, radish, and dill.
3. Spread a layer of vegan cream cheese on each wrap.
4. Top with a thin layer of carrot lox and equal amounts of the shiitake mushroom and radish mixture.
5. Roll the wrap tightly and cut into 8 pieces.
6. Place on a baking sheet and bake for 20 minutes or until crisp.

**Nutrition information: Per Serving: Calories 271, Total Fat 6.2g, Protein 8g, Carbohydrate 45.3g, Fiber 5.8g, Sodium 376mg.**

## 75. Vegan Green Dragon Roll with Asparagus and Avocado

This vegan green dragon roll with asparagus and avocado is a delicious and healthy combination of flavors. It's made with sushi seaweed, is gluten-free, and is a great way to enjoy sushi without consuming fish.
Serving: 4
Preparation Time: 10 minutes
Ready Time: 25 minutes

**Ingredients:**
1 cup cooked asparagus, cut into 2-inch pieces
1 cup cooked sushi rice
1/4 teaspoon sea salt
4 sheets nori (dried seaweed)
1/4 avocado, sliced
1/4 cup vegan mayonnaise
1 teaspoon toasted sesame oil

**Instructions:**
1. Begin by preparing the sushi rolls. Mix the cooked sushi rice with the salt and blend in a medium bowl.

2. Place a sheet of seaweed on a bamboo rolling mat. Wet your hands with cold water and spread a thin layer of rice across the seaweed, leaving about an inch on both long sides.

3. Place the asparagus in the center of the rice. Spread the avocado slices on top.

4. Carefully lift one of the long sides of the seaweed and begin rolling into a log. Seal the seaweed by pressing it down firmly.

5. Cut the log into four even circles. Place the rolls on a plate and serve.

6. Drizzle with vegan mayonnaise and toasted sesame oil.

**Nutrition information: Serving Size: 4 rolls, Calories: 228, Protein: 3g, Fat: 11g, Carbohydrates: 31g, Sodium: 468mg**

## 76. Vegan Spicy Vegetable and Avocado Roll with Radish

Enjoy the flavors of nature with this vegan-friendly spicy vegetable avocado roll with radish. Made with vegan-friendly Ingredients like tamari, sesame oil, and avocado, it is a healthy snack or light meal that can be enjoyed by those of all diets.

Serving: 4 servings

Preparation Time: 25 minutes

Ready Time: 45 minutes

**Ingredients:**
- 2 teaspoons olive oil
- 8 ounces mixed mushrooms, thinly sliced
- 2 cloves garlic, minced
- 4 green onions, thinly sliced
- 2 tablespoons tamari
- 2 tablespoons toasted sesame oil
- 2 medium avocados, pitted and cubed
- 4 nori sheets
- 8-10 radishes, thinly sliced
- Pickled ginger (optional)

**Instructions:**
1. In a medium skillet, heat the olive oil over medium-high heat.

Add the mushrooms and garlic and cook for 4-5 minutes, stirring occasionally, until tender.
Add the green onions and cook for another minute.
Add the tamari and sesame oil and stir to combine. Remove from heat and set aside.
2. Place each sheet of nori on a flat work surface and spread some of the mushroom filling over the sheet.
Top with a layer of avocado cubes and radish slices.
Roll up the nori sheet into a tight cylinder and place, seam-side-down, on a plate.
Repeat with remaining sheets.
3. Serve with pickled ginger, if desired.

**Nutrition information:**
Calories: 207, Total Fat: 13.6g, Saturated Fat: 2.4g, Cholesterol: 0mg, Sodium: 429mg, Total Carbohydrates: 17.8g, Fiber: 7.3g, Net Carbs: 10.5g, Sugars: 3.3g, Protein: 6.3g.


# 77. Vegan Tempura Avocado and Cucumber Roll with Carrot Lox

This vegan tempura avocado and cucumber roll with carrot lox is a delicious and healthful appetizer or entrée that is bursting with flavor. This easy-to-make vegan meal features hearty, nutrient-packed carrots and fresh, crunchy cucumbers that are tempura-fried and wrapped in a zesty avocado roll for a flavorful and satisfying meal.
Serving: 4
Preparation Time: 10 minutes
Ready Time: 25 minutes

**Ingredients:**
- 1 carrot, julienned
- 1 cup cold water
- 2 tablespoons agar-agar flakes
- 2 avocados, halved and pitted
- 2 tablespoons freshly squeezed lime juice
- 1 teaspoon sea salt
- ½ cup tempura batter

- 2 cucumbers, julienned
- 2 tablespoons nori flakes
- 1 tablespoon sesame seeds

**Instructions:**
1. In a small saucepan, combine the carrot, water, and agar-agar flakes, and bring to a boil over medium heat. Simmer for about 8 minutes, stirring occasionally, until the carrot is fully cooked. Remove from heat and drain.
2. In a medium bowl, combine the avocado, lime juice, and salt. Mash together until a paste is formed.
3. Place the tempura batter in a small bowl. Scoop out about 2 tablespoons of the avocado paste and spread it out onto a plate or tray. Place the julienned cucumber on top of the avocado and press down gently.
4. Dip each cucumber-avocado roll into the tempura batter and then deep fry in a large pot of oil at 375 degrees F until golden brown, about 4 minutes. Place the rolls on a paper towel-lined plate to drain.
5. Sprinkle the top of each roll with nori flakes and sesame seeds.

**Nutrition information:**
Calories: 158, Fat: 9g, Saturated fat: 1g, Sodium: 298mg, Carbohydrates: 20g, Fiber: 5g, Protein: 3g, Sugar: 2g

## 78. Vegan Mango and Sweet Potato Roll with Radish

This vegan mango and sweet potato roll with radish is a healthy, vegan-friendly recipe. It features a flavorful combination of sweet potatoes, mango, and radishes, all rolled into a delicious wrap. It's simple and easy to make, and can be enjoyed by people of all dietary preferences.
Serving: 2 rolls
Preparation Time: 10 minutes
Ready Time: 15 minutes

**Ingredients:**
-1/2 large sweet potato, diced small
-1/2 medium mango, diced small
-2 radishes, diced small

-2 large burrito-size tortilla wraps
- 2 tablespoons vegan mayonnaise
-1 teaspoon fresh lime juice

**Instructions:**
1. In a large skillet over medium heat, cook the diced sweet potatoes for 5 to 8 minutes, stirring occasionally.
2. After the sweet potatoes have cooked for a few minutes, add the diced mango and radishes to the skillet. Cook for an additional 5 minutes.
3. Place the tortillas on a flat surface and spread 1 tablespoon of vegan mayonnaise on each.
4. Top each tortilla with the sweet potato, mango, and radish mix.
5. Drizzle each wrap with the lime juice and fold into a roll.
6. Slice each roll in half, and enjoy!

**Nutrition information (per serving): 266 calories, 11g fat, 39g carbohydrates, 5g protein.**


## 79. Vegan Philadelphia Roll with Carrot Lox and Avocado

Satisfy your sushi cravings with this delicious and vegan-friendly Philadelphia roll. This artisanal vegan sushi roll is filled with carrot lox, cream cheese, and avocado, and is a perfect appetizer or entree.
Serving: Makes one 8-piece sushi roll
Preparationtime: 10 minutes
Readytime: 10 minutes

**Ingredients:**
4 sheets of nori seaweed
1 ½ cups cooked sushi rice
3 tablespoons vegan cream cheese
1 large carrot, julienned
¼ cup coconut milk
1 tablespoon agave nectar
½ teaspoon liquid smoke
2 avocados, thinly sliced

**Instructions:**

1. In a medium bowl, combine the coconut milk, agave nectar, and liquid smoke. Add the julienned carrot to the marinade and set aside.
2. Place a nori sheet on a bamboo mat, and spread 1/3 cup of prepared sushi rice over it.
3. Layer cream cheese and the marinated carrot on top.
4. Place avocado slices on top.
5. Roll the sushi, using the bamboo mat to shape it. Cut into 8 pieces.

**Nutrition information: Per 8-piece roll: 398 calories, 16g fat, 57g carbohydrates, 6g protein, 7g fibre, 91mg sodium**

# 80. Vegan Peanut Avocado and Cucumber Roll with Carrot Lox

This vibrant, vegan and gluten-free roll is filled with a creamy, zesty and light flavor combination of avocado, peanut butter, and cucumber. Carrots are smoked in the oven for a smoky salmon texture.

Serving: 6-8 rolls
Preparation time: 15 minutes
Ready time: 40 minutes

**Ingredients:**
- 5 to 6 carrots
- Sea salt
- 5 tablespoons of oil
- 2 tablespoons of liquid smoke
- 1 avocado mashed
- 1 tablespoon of peanut butter
- 1 tablespoon of lemon juice
- 1/4 cup of chopped cucumber
- 6-8 sheets of moistened rice paper

**Instructions:**
1. Preheat the oven to 375°F.
2. Cut the carrots into long thin strips resembling smoked salmon. Place the carrot strips on a lined baking sheet.

3. Drizzle with oil, sprinkle with sea salt and liquid smoke and rub to evenly distribute it all.
4. Bake for 25 minutes.
5. In a bowl, combine the mashed avocado, peanut butter, lemon juice, and cucumber.
6. Dip the sheets of rice paper into warm water until soft and supple.
7. Place a sheet of rice paper down on a flat surface. Place a spoonful of the avocado mixture and spread it along the edge of the roll.
8. Top with a few pieces of roasted carrots.
9. Roll like a burrito, tucking in the edges while rolling.
10. Cut into discs and serve.

**Nutrition information:**
Calories - 150, Fat - 10g, Protein - 2.5g, Carbs - 13.5g, Fiber - 4.5g, Sugar - 5g, Sodium - 20mg.

# 81. Vegan Spicy Tofu Tempura and Asparagus Roll with Radish

This vegan spicy tofu tempura and asparagus roll with radish is served up as an appetizer or part of a meal. Enjoy this delicious, healthy and vegan snack.
Serving: 2 servings
Preparation Time: 15 minutes
Ready Time: 15 minutes

**Ingredients:**
-1/2 packet of firm tofu
-2 tsp of olive oil
-2 cloves of garlic
-1/2 tsp of chili flakes
-2 asparagus spears
-1/2 a punnet of radishes, thinly sliced
-50g tempura batter mix

**Instructions:**
1. Heat the olive oil in a small pan and add the garlic and chili flakes.

2. Cut the tofu into thin strips and add to the pan, cooking until lightly golden.
3. Cut the asparagus into thin strips and add to the pan.
4. Cook for a few minutes until the vegetables are lightly cooked.
5. Prepare the tempura batter mix according to the packet instructions.
6. Dip the cooked vegetable strips into the batter and fry in hot oil for a few minutes until golden and crisp.
7. Arrange the cooked vegetable strips on a plate with the radish slices.
8. Roll all of the vegetables together with the radish slices in the middle and serve.

**Nutrition information:**
Calories: 88
Fat: 3g
Carbohydrates: 5g
Protein: 8g
Sugar: 2g

## 82. Vegan Crunchy Spicy Mayo and Shiitake Mushroom Roll with Carrot Lox

Vegan Crunchy Spicy Mayo and Shiitake Mushroom Roll with Carrot Lox is a flavorful and nutritious meal suitable for any occasion. Served hot off the stove, this meal offers a unique combination of flavor and texture that you won't soon forget.
Serving: 4-6
Preparation Time: 20 minutes
Ready Time: 45 minutes

**Ingredients:**
- 4 cups Shiitake mushrooms, thinly sliced
- 2 carrots, julienned
- Mayonnaise
- Spicy Sriracha sauce
- Salt and pepper
- 2 tablespoons olive oil or vegan butter
- 1/2 cup breadcrumbs

**Instructions:**
1. Preheat oven to 350 degrees.
2. Spread the sliced shiitake mushrooms and julienned carrots in an even layer in a roasting pan. Drizzle with olive oil or vegan butter, then sprinkle with salt and pepper. Roast in preheated oven for 20 minutes, stirring once halfway through.
3. In a small bowl, mix mayonnaise and Sriracha to create a spicy mayo.
4. When the vegetables have finished roasting, spoon a generous layer of the mayonnaise mixture onto a large plate. Place the shiitakes and carrots on top of the mayonnaise, then sprinkle with breadcrumbs.
5. Roll up the veggies tightly in the plate and chill for about 25 minutes.
6. Slice the vegan roll into thin discs and serve atop a bed of salad greens, or as a side dish.

**Nutrition information:**
Calories: 160
Carbs: 16g
Fat: 7g
Protein: 3g
Sodium: 400mg

# 83. Vegan Teriyaki Portobello and Cucumber Roll with Radish

This vegan teriyaki portobello and cucumber roll with radish is a light and nutritious meal that is sure to please vegetarians and those who are looking for something different. Delightfully flavorful and healthy, this delicious dish is easy to make and sure to create smiles.
Serving: Serves 2
Preparation Time: 10 minutes
Ready Time: 30 minutes

**Ingredients:**
- 2 large portobello mushrooms, sliced
- 2 tablespoons low-sodium teriyaki sauce
- 1 cucumber, cut into thin strips
- 2 radishes, cut into thin slices
- 1 teaspoon sesame oil

- 1 teaspoon minced garlic
- 1 tablespoon rice vinegar

**Instructions:**
1. Preheat oven to 375°F.
2. In a bowl, mix together the teriyaki sauce, sesame oil, minced garlic, and rice vinegar.
3. Dip each mushroom slice in the teriyaki sauce mixture.
4. Place the mushroom slices on a baking sheet coated with cooking spray. Bake for 10 minutes.
5. On a serving plate, spread one mushroom slice. Place a row of cucumber strips on top of it.
6. Top the cucumbers with radish slices.
7. Place the second mushroom slice on top, creating a roll.
8. Drizzle remaining teriyaki sauce mix over the top.

**Nutrition information:**
Serving Size: 1 roll
Calories: 40
Protein: 5g
Carbs: 7g
Fiber: 2g
Fat: 1g

## 84. Vegan Tempura Asparagus and Avocado Roll with Carrot Lox

Enjoy this delicious vegan tempura asparagus and avocado roll with carrot lox! This fusion-style entree is packed with nutrition and flavor - it's sure to become a family favorite. Servings: 4 Preparation Time: 15 minutes Ready Time: 30 minutes

**Ingredients:**
• 2 bunches of asparagus • 2 avocados • 8 sheets of nori • 8 tablespoons of vegan tempura batter mix • 2 cups of cold water • ½ cup of grated carrots • ½ cup of vegan mayo • 2 tablespoons of liquid smoke

**Instructions:**

1. Preheat a large saucepan filled with vegetable oil to 375°F.

2. Cut off the asparagus ends and cut the remaining piece into 2-inch pieces. Peel and thinly slice the avocado into strips.

3. In a medium bowl, mix the tempura batter mix and cold water until it's evenly combined.

4. Dip the asparagus pieces into the batter and carefully lower them into the heated oil. Fry for 2-3 minutes until golden brown, transfer to a paper-towel-lined plate.

5. On a sushi mat, lay down one sheet of nori and spread 1/2 tablespoon of mayo evenly over the nori. Then, top with an even layer of grated carrots and fried asparagus pieces.

6. Place one strip of avocado next to the vegetables, then evenly spread 1 tablespoon of mayo on top. Roll the sushi mat tightly away from you, making sure to press it firmly. Cut each sushi roll into 6 pieces.

7. In a small bowl, mix together the carrots and remainder vegan mayo with the liquid smoke.

8. Garnish each piece of tempura asparagus and avocado roll with a small spoonful of the carrot lox.

**Nutrition information: Per serving: 348 calories, 24g fat, 15g protein, 25g carbohydrates, 8g fiber**

## 85. Vegan Mango and Jalapeno Roll with Radish and Cucumber

This vegan mango and jalapeno roll is the perfect light and refreshing summer snack. With crunchy cucumber, radishes, and sweet mango wrapped in a jalapeno-infused wrap, it's sure to be a crowd favorite!

Serving: Makes 6-8 rolls

Preparation Time: 10 minutes

Ready Time: 10 minutes

**Ingredients:**
- 8 inch rice paper wraps
- 2 mangos, diced
- 1 jalapeno, finely diced
- 1/4 cup thinly sliced radishes
- 1-2 cucumbers, julienned

**Instructions:**
1. In a large bowl, combine the diced mango, jalapeno, radishes, and cucumber. Mix until well combined.
2. Fill a shallow bowl with warm water. Working one at a time, dip the rice paper wraps in the water and allow to soften for 30-45 seconds.
3. Lay the wrap on a board or plate and fill the center with a generous amount of the mango-jalapeno mixture.
4. Fold the bottom of the wrap over the filling and tuck tightly. Fold in the sides and roll the wrap, tucking in as you go.

**Nutrition information: Per Serving (1/6 of recipe): 128 calories; 0 g total fat; 0 g saturated fat; 0 g trans fat; 0 mg cholesterol; 337 mg sodium; 29 g total carbohydrate; 10 g dietary fiber; 15 g sugars; 3 g protein.**

## 86. Vegan BBQ Mushroom and Cucumber Roll with Carrot Lox

This vegan BBQ Mushroom and Cucumber Roll with Carrot Lox is a flavorful and vegan-friendly sushi roll filled with delicious Ingredients.
Serving: 6 rolls
Preparation Time: 25 minutes
Ready Time: 45 minutes

**Ingredients:**
- 1/2 carrot, cut into matchsticks
- 2 tablespoons olive oil
- 1/2 teaspoon liquid smoke
- 1 teaspoon minced garlic
- 1 teaspoon smoked paprika
- 1/4 cup tamari
- 2 tablespoons maple syrup
- 2 tablespoons apple cider vinegar
- 6 portobello mushrooms, cut into thin strips
- 1 large cucumber, cut into thin slices
- 2 tablespoons vegan mayonnaise
- 2 tablespoons sesame seeds

• 1 sheet nori

**Instructions:**
1. Preheat oven to 375°F.
2. In a bowl, combine carrots, olive oil, liquid smoke, garlic, smoked paprika, tamari, maple syrup, and apple cider vinegar. Mix to combine.
3. Arrange carrots on a baking sheet and bake for 25 minutes until carrots are tender.
4. Meanwhile, cut the portobello mushrooms into thin strips and slice cucumber.
5. In a small bowl, mix vegan mayonnaise and sesame seeds.
6. Lay nori sheet on a flat surface. Spread the sesame mayo mixture on the nori.
7. Arrange the bbq carrots, mushroom strips, and cucumber slices in a line in the middle of the nori.
8. Starting at the end closest to you, roll the nori, tucking in the Ingredients as you go.
9. Slice into 6 rolls and serve.

**Nutrition information: Per roll: 100 calories, 8g fat, 6g carbohydrates, 2g protein.**


## 87. Avocado and Radish Roll with Carrot Lox and Bell Pepper

Avocado and Radish Roll with Carrot Lox and Bell Pepper is a healthy, vegan, plant-based dish that is great for any occasion. The combination of flavors and colors make it a beautiful appetizer or light lunch.
Serving: 4
Preparation Time: 10 minutes
Ready Time: 10 minutes


**Ingredients:**
- Avocado: 2
- Radishes: 4-5
- Carrot lox: 1 cup
- Red bell pepper: 1
- lemon: 1

- Greens (optional): 2 cups
- Cashews (optional): 2 tbsp
- Salt and pepper: to taste

**Instructions:**
1. In a medium mixing bowl, mash the avocado and set aside.
2. Slice the radishes and bell pepper as thin as possible and set aside.
3. Heat a non-stick pan over medium heat and add the carrot lox. Cook for 3 minutes, stirring occasionally.
4. Add the lemon juice and cook for another 2 minutes until lox is cooked through.
5. Take four plates and start to assemble the rolls by spreading the mashed avocado on a plate. Add the radishes, carrot lox and bell pepper and top with greens and cashews. Sprinkle with salt and pepper to taste.
6. Serve the rolls with a side of greens and some avocado slices for extra creaminess.

**Nutrition information:**
Calories: 120 kcal
Carbohydrates: 8 g
Protein: 2 g
Fat: 10 g
Sugar: 3 g
Fiber: 4 g

## 88. Vegan Dynamite Spicy Mayo and Sweet Potato Roll with Radish

Get ready for a delicious roll for the perfect combination of sweet and spicy! This vegan dish features sweet potatoes, spicy mayo, and radish for a tasty treat that's perfect anytime.
Serving: 4
Preparation Time: 35 minutes
Ready Time: 45 minutes

**Ingredients:**
2 large sweet potatoes
1/4 cup vegan mayonnaise

1 teaspoon Sriracha sauce
5 small radish, thinly sliced

**Instructions:**
1. Preheat oven to 425°F (220°C).
2. Slice the sweet potatoes into 1/2-inch thick slices. Place on a baking sheet and bake for 15 minutes.
3. In a small bowl, mix the mayonnaise, Sriracha sauce, and radish slices.
4. Spread the mayonnaise mixture over the sweet potato slices and bake for 15 minutes.
5. Serve the Vegan Dynamite Spicy Mayo and Sweet Potato Roll with Radish warm.

**Nutrition information (Per Serving): Calories: 81, Fat: 4g, Saturated Fat: 0g, Cholesterol: 0mg, Sodium: 138mg, Carbohydrates: 11g, Fiber: 2g, Sugar: 6g, Protein: 1g**

## 89. Vegan Teriyaki Tofu and Bell Pepper Roll with Carrot Lox

Enjoy a delicious and vegan twist on a classic Asian dish with this Vegan Teriyaki Tofu and Bell Pepper Roll with Carrot Lox.
Serving: 2-3
Preparation Time: 15 minutes
Ready Time: 30 minutes

**Ingredients:**
- 10 oz extra firm tofu
- 1 tbsp coconut aminos
- 2 garlic cloves, minced
- 2 tbsp maple syrup
- 2 tbsp coconut oil
- 2 bell peppers, diced
- 3 carrots, grated
- 2 tbsp fresh lemon juice

**Instructions:**

1. In a medium bowl, whisk together coconut aminos, garlic, and maple syrup and set aside.
2. Heat a large skillet over medium heat and add coconut oil. Once melted, add the diced bell peppers and cook for 2-3 minutes.
3. Add tofu to the skillet and pour the teriyaki sauce over top. Stir to combine and cook for 10 minutes.
4. To assemble the roll, spread grated carrots onto a plate. Place the tofu and bell pepper mixture into the middle of the carrots and roll. Finish off with a drizzle of fresh lemon juice.

**Nutrition information: Calories: 201, Fat: 10g, Carbs: 19g, Protein: 9g**

## 90. Vegan Shiitake Mushroom and Avocado Roll with Radish and Cucumber

For a light and healthy vegan snack or meal, try this vegan shiitake mushroom and avocado roll with radish and cucumber. This easy and tasty roll-up is bursting with flavor and nutritious vitamins and minerals.
Serving: 1
Preparation Time: 10 minutes
Ready time: 10 minutes

**Ingredients:**
- 2 sheets of nori
- 3-5 shiitake mushrooms, chopped
- 1/2 avocado, diced
- 1/4 cup radish, julienned
- 1/4 cup cucumber, julienned

**Instructions:**
1. Cut two sheets of nori into four equal rectangles, for a total of eight.
2. Place the chopped mushrooms, avocado, radish, and cucumber in a bowl and mix together.
3. Place a spoonful of the mixture into the center of each rectangle of nori, and then roll the nori up around it until it forms a tight roll.
4. Cut each roll into 1-inch pieces and serve.

**Nutrition information:**
Calories: 97, Total Fat: 6g, Saturated Fat: 1g, Trans Fat: 0g, Cholesterol: 0mg, Sodium: 8mg, Total carbs: 6g, Fiber: 3g, Sugar: 0g, Protein: 3g.

95

## 91. Vegan Spicy Peanut and Cucumber Roll with Carrot Lox and Bell Pepper

These vegan spicy peanut and cucumber rolls with carrot lox and bell pepper are an easy and flavorful meal that's perfect for lunch or dinner.
Serving: Makes 4-6 rolls
Preparation time: 10 minutes
Ready time: 20 minutes

**Ingredients:**
- 1 carrot, julienned
- 2 tablespoons tamari
- 1 bell pepper, julienned
- 1/4 cup peanuts
- 1/4 cup peanut butter
- 1 tbsp Sriracha
- 2-3 cucumbers, cut into long strips

**Instructions:**
1. Preheat oven to 400°F.
2. Spread the julienned carrots onto a baking sheet.
3. Drizzle with tamari and bake for 10 minutes.
4. In a small bowl, mix together peanut butter, peanuts, and Sriracha.
5. Lay out cucumber strips on a cutting board.
6. Spread the peanut butter mixture onto one end of the cucumber strips.
7. Top with bell pepper and carrot lox.
8. Roll tightly.
9. Cut in half, and serve.

**Nutrition information:**
Calories: 95
Carbs: 9g
Fat: 5g
Protein: 4g

# 92. Vegan Cucumber and Bell Pepper Roll with Carrot Lox and Avocado

Vegan cucumber and bell pepper roll with carrot lox and avocado is a delicious vegan sushi-style dish. The combination of nutritious vegetables and vegan protein makes it a balanced and light dinner option.
Serving: 4
Preparation Time: 15 minutes
Ready Time: 15 minutes

**Ingredients:**
- 2 small cucumbers, thinly sliced
- 2 bell peppers, cut into thin strips
- ½ cup vegan cream cheese
- 2 tablespoons fresh dill, chopped
- 2 tablespoons nutritional yeast
- 1 teaspoon garlic powder
- ½ teaspoon onion powder
- 2 carrots, peeled and thinly sliced
- 1 avocado, peeled and sliced

**Instructions:**
1. In a small bowl, combine the vegan cream cheese, dill, nutritional yeast, garlic powder, and onion powder. Mix well to combine.
2. Lay out a slice of cucumber and spread a thin layer of the cream cheese mixture over the top.
3. Lay a strip of bell pepper and a slice of carrot on top of the cream cheese.
4. Roll the cucumber tightly and place on a plate. Repeat until all of the Ingredients have been used.
5. Place the avocado slices on top of the rolls and serve immediately.

**Nutrition information: Per serving: Calories: 115, Fat: 7g, Carbohydrates: 10g, Protein: 4g, Fiber: 3g, Sodium: 119mg**

# 93. Vegan California Roll with Mango, Avocado, and Radish

This vegan California roll with mango, avocado, and radish is a healthy and flavorful alternative to the classic sushi. Servings: 4 Prep Time: 30 minutes Ready Time: 30 minutes

**Ingredients:**
 2 cups cooked sushi rice, 2 Nori sheets, 1/2 mango, diced, 1/2 avocado, diced, 1/2 radish, grated, 2 tablespoons white sesame seeds

**Instructions:**
 1. Create sushi rice by combining cooked sushi rice, 1 tablespoon white sesame seeds, and 1 tablespoon of salt. Mix until combined.
2. Place 1 Nori sheet onto a sushi rolling mat. Spread 1 cup of sushi rice onto the Nori sheet in a thin layer, being careful not to leave gaps in between the rice.
3. Place the mango, avocado, and radish onto the rice in long rows.
4. Place the other Nori sheet on top of the filling and press the layers together firmly.
5. Using the sushi rolling mat, begin to roll the California Roll tightly. The more times you roll, the more compact the sushi will become.
6. Using a knife, cut the roll into eight pieces.
7. Turn the pieces onto the plate and garnish with the remaining white sesame seeds.
8. Serve and enjoy!

**Nutrition information: One serving of California Roll contains approximately 120 calories, 2 grams of fat, 21 grams of carbohydrates, 2 grams of dietary fiber, 8 grams of sugar, and 2 grams of protein.**


# 94. Vegan Teriyaki Jackfruit and Asparagus Roll with Radish

This vegan teriyaki jackfruit and asparagus roll with radish is a flavorful and nutritious meal made with only a few simple Ingredients. Fresh and healthy, this dish is sure to become a staple in your home.

Serving: Makes 4 rolls
Preparation Time: 10 minutes
Ready Time: 20 minutes

**Ingredients:**
- ¼ cup vegan teriyaki sauce
- 1 can of jackfruit, drained
- 4 asparagus, stems removed and cut into quarters
- 1 radish, thinly sliced into rounds
- 4 sheets of nori

**Instructions:**
1. Preheat oven to 375°F.
2. In a small bowl, mix together the vegan teriyaki sauce and jackfruit.
3. Take one sheet of nori and spread about 2 tablespoons of jackfruit mixture on the sheet, top evenly with asparagus and radish slices.
4. Roll the nori and place on a baking sheet seam side down.
5. Repeat step 3 two more times.
6. Bake rolls for about 10 minutes.
7. Serve and enjoy.

**Nutrition information (per roll):**
- Calories: 79
- Protein: 4 g
- Total Fat: 1 g
- Saturated Fat: 0 g
- Cholesterol: 0 mg
- Carbs: 14 g
- Fiber: 2 g
- Sugar: 7 g
- Sodium: 711 mg

## 95. Vegan Tempura Shiitake Mushroom and Cucumber Roll with Carrot Lox

Get ready for a new recipe that will impress everyone! This Vegan Tempura Shiitake Mushroom and Cucumber Roll with Carrot Lox is a creative and delicious dish that will please vegans and meat-eaters alike.

Serving: 2-3
Preparation time: 35 minutes
Ready time: 45 minutes

**Ingredients:**
-1 cup flour
-1 cup cold soda water
-1 teaspoon baking powder
-1 teaspoon sea salt
-4 ounces of shiitake mushrooms
-3 ounces of cucumber
-2 ounces of carrot lox
-Oil for frying

**Instructions:**
1. In a medium sized bowl, mix together the flour, soda water, baking powder, and sea salt to make a normalized tempura batter.
2. Slice the shiitake mushrooms, cucumber, and carrot lox into thin strips.
3. Dip the mushroom, cucumber, and lox strips into the tempura batter and Coat well.
4. Heat the oil in a large skillet.
5. Carefully place the strips in the hot oil and fry until golden brown.
6. Remove from heat and let cool.
7. To assemble the rolls, place a cucumber and mushroom strip in the center of a piece of lox then roll it up.
8. Serve warm.

**Nutrition information: Each serving of Tempura Shiitake Mushroom and Cucumber Roll with Carrot Lox contains approximately 200 calories, 8 grams of fat, 26 grams of carbohydrates, 3 grams of fiber, and 6 grams of protein.**

## 96. Vegan Mango and Cucumber Roll with Radish, Avocado, and Bell Pepper

This vegan mango and cucumber roll with radish, avocado, and bell pepper is a light and healthy meal that's perfect for lunches or any time you want something fresh and light.

Serving: 8

Preparation time: 10 minutes

Ready time: 30 minutes

**Ingredients:**
- 1 cucumber
- 1 ripe mango
- 4-5 radishes
- 2 lemons
- 1 bell pepper
- 1 diced avocado
- freshly chopped mint
- Himalayan pink salt

**Instructions:**
1. Slice the cucumber into thin strips and lay them flat on a plate or cutting board.
2. Peel, pit, and cube the mango. Sprinkle with juice from the lemon and set aside.
3. Slice the radishes into thin slices and dice the bell pepper.
4. Spread the cucumber slices with diced avocado and top with the radish and bell pepper slices.
5. Sprinkle with freshly chopped mint and Himalayan pink salt.
6. Roll the cucumber slices up with the other Ingredients and secure with a toothpick.
7. Serve the rolls with the cubed mango and a wedge of lemon for squeezing.

**Nutrition information:**
Calories: 65 kcal

Carbs: 15 g

Protein: 1 g

Fats: 3 g

Saturated Fat: 0 g

Cholesterol: 0 mg

Sodium: 119 mg

Potassium: 387 mg

Sugar: 9 g


## 97. Vegan Spicy Mayo and Avocado Roll with Carrot Lox, Cucumber, and Jalapeno

Enjoy this flavorful and vegan-friendly spicy mayo and avocado roll with carrot lox, cucumber, and jalapeno.
Serving: Makes 4 rolls.
Preparation time: 10 minutes
Ready time: 10 minutes

**Ingredients:**
- 1 ripe avocado
- 1/4 teaspoon ground cumin
- 1/4 teaspoon garlic powder
- Juice of 1/2 lemon
- 4 Nori (seaweed) sheets
- 4 teaspoons vegan mayonnaise
- 1 carrot, julienned
- 2 jalapenos, thinly sliced
- 1 cucumber, julienned

**Instructions:**
1. Begin by mashing the avocado in a small bowl.
2. Add the cumin, garlic powder, and lemon juice to the bowl. Mash everything together until well-combined.
3. Set aside four Nori (seaweed) sheets.
4. Spread each Nori sheet with 1 teaspoon of vegan mayonnaise.
5. Divide up the mashed avocado evenly over the four Nori sheets.
6. Top each sheet with the julienned carrot, cucumber, and jalapenos.
7. Starting from the edge closest to you, begin rolling up the Nori sheet tightly.
8. Slice the roll in half and serve immediately.

**Nutrition information: Calories- 143, Fat- 10 g, Carbohydrates- 6 g, Protein- 3.30 g, Sugar- 1.15 g, Sodium- 37 mg**

# CONCLUSION

Sustainable Sushi: 97 Delicious Plant-Based Recipes is a comprehensive guide to making delicious vegan sushi dishes without sacrificing any of the flavor of traditional sushi. In this book, author Ginger Hahn offers an array of recipes that swap out seafood, for vegan ingredients that are equally delicious while being ethical, sustainable, and healthful. From salads and futomaki to sushi rolls and desserts, this book is sure to satisfy all cravings.

With Hahn's expertise and eye for detail, each recipe is carefully crafted to ensure success — even for first-time sushi makers. From selecting the right ingredients to clever twists, Hahn provides her readers with everything they need to make delicious and nutritious plant-based sushi, which in turn can also serve as an ongoing source of inspiration for creating more vegan recipes.

Every recipe in Sustainable Sushi: 97 Delicious Plant-Based Recipes is easy to follow and includes clear instructions that can be followed either by the novice or the expert. Hahn also provides helpful advice before each recipe, such as what sushi-making supplies are necessary, storage tips, and food safety advice. Additionally, all recipes are gluten-free, which is a bonus for those with allergies and sensitivities.

The contents of this cookbook are divided into seven sections: Introduction, Salad and Appetizers, Futomaki, Sushi Rolls and Pizza, 6 With Rice, Specialty Rolls, and Desserts. Every recipe features a wealth of tips, techniques, and mouthwatering photographs that will help to inspire more creative vegan recipes. Each recipe is accompanied by an explanation of its origin, ingredients, and detailed instructions, making it easy to recreate the dishes.

Sustainable Sushi: 97 Delicious Plant-Based Recipes is a valuable resource for those looking to create delicious, sustainable vegan dishes. All of the recipes in this book are not only healthy for the planet, but also for your body. Additionally, all of the recipes can easily be adapted for vegans and vegetarians alike, making it a go-to cookbook for those who want to adopt a plant-based diet.

At the end of the day, the key to a successful vegan diet is preparing meals that are delicious, sustainable, and nutritious. With Sustainable Sushi: 97 Delicious Plant-Based Recipes, you can make delicious, vegan sushi dishes that still satisfy the cravings of traditional sushi. The recipes in this book are only limited by your own creativity, and it's sure to leave you craving more.